CIRCUSES, BEATS & BLENHEIMS

First published in 2005 by

WOODFIELD PUBLISHING
Bognor Regis, West Sussex, England
www.woodfieldpublishing.com

ISBN 1-903953-98-7

Circuses, Beats & Blenheims

Memoirs of a Wartime Bomber Pilot

GORDON SHACKLETON

Woodfield

The Author, newly qualified as a pilot, 1941.

Contents

Portrait of the author in uniform, 1943.

Introduction

From the age of about eight I had set my sights on two ambitions: to drive a train and to fly an aeroplane. Now, 12 years later, I was about to do the latter. Small Miles Magister aeroplanes were used for our training and, with a great feeling of excitement, I climbed into the back seat, my instructor already in the front. How strange, everything seemed, so different from the motor cars and lorries which I had driven since the age of 16. The instrument panel was extremely simple, I remember, with little more than an airspeed indicator, altimeter and petrol gauge, but it appeared complicated to me. From my seat at the rear it was hidden from view anyway, so upon taking over from my instructor I was told to use the horizon to keep straight and to look down at the ground to get our direction.

At first, all I could think about was that I would never be able to master keeping the aircraft straight instead of jerking it up and down, while maintaining level wings seemed virtually impossible. As soon as I corrected one error I would make another, there was such a lot to think about at once... but suddenly it all came together and I was actually flying an aeroplane!

Following my disappointment at not having been chosen for a fighter squadron I calmly accepted being sent to fly Blenheims. At the time, it never occurred to me that these light bombers were already obsolete when I joined 114 Squadron and that consequently anyone flying in them would be exposed to increased danger. To Leading Aircraftsman Shackleton they were modern planes and a huge step up from the Magister. Due to having an enclosed cockpit the Blenheim was far more comfortable than my first type of training aircraft, but that was only relative, as it had poor heating and no soundproofing so was cold and noisy. Visibility also took some getting used to at first, as although when airborne one could see all around, on the ground one's vision was restricted to either side only, the view in front being obscured by the engine.

During our Initial Training we kept warm in the Magister's open cockpit by wearing a Sidcot flying suit over our battle-dress, however, in the Blenheim, apart from the mandatory helmet, flying boots and gloves, we could wear our battle-dress only and this was a great relief as wearing the two at the same time felt heavy and awkward. Thus we kept our Sidcot suits just for use on cold days. There was, of course, always some heat seeping into the cockpit from the engines, which was welcome when we climbed higher and the outside temperature dropped. Fitted with numerous under-used zips, a Sidcot suit was so roomy that an extra, padded suit could be worn in between it and one's battledress for high altitude flying. It was also equipped with wiring, which could be plugged into the planes heating system when one got up to around 20,000 feet, which kept out the cold most effectively.

As we progressed through our basic training, if any trainee pilot was not 'up to scratch' our instructor would report the matter to the flight commander. The FC would then take the pupil up himself and if the fellow still got a 'thumbs down' he was taken off the course and posted elsewhere. Chaps who could not make it as pilots usually finished up at gunnery or navigation schools to become successful and extremely useful wireless-operator/air gunners or navigator/bomb-aimers. Those of us who were left were driven on by such enthusiasm that in spite of a few crashes (no fatalities, thank goodness) we were all eager for the move from Magisters to Oxfords and Blenheims when the time came.

Oxfords were twin-engined with enclosed cockpits, so bridged the gap to flying Blenheims. Also, being more manoeuvrable and not as fast as the latter made them ideal for that purpose while with their slower takeoff and landing speed they gave the pilot time to adjust his vision.

While on Oxfords we got our first taste of night flying, which in spite of only being 'circuits and landings' gave us a preview of what was to come. Upon transferring to Blenheims we had to get used to an aeroplane which was more powerful by far than an Oxford, with a takeoff speed of 70 to 80 miles per hour, while the latter became airborne at 65 miles per hour.

In those days there was no ceremony for getting one's pilot's wings, just a notice which appeared with Daily Routine Orders (DROs) saying, for example, that LACs Shackleton, Jones and Bloggs had been awarded their wings. Out of the 20 to 30 would-be pilots in my group only six of us received our wings – the most exciting day of our young lives.

A typical daylight operation

Before breakfast each morning we would go to the notice board to check the DROs and if there was to be an Op that day, they would read, for example: *"briefing will take place at 0700 hrs."*

Following breakfast, we pilots would go to our briefing room for instructions from the squadron leader while our navigator/bomb aimers and wireless operator/air-gunners had their own separate briefings, the former by the senior Pilot's Observer (navigator) and the latter by the Senior Pilot's Rear Gunner or Gunnery Leader. In the pilots' briefing room, we would be informed as to whether we should be going alone or in 'vic' formations, each with an average of 12 planes, and whether we would be flying at high or low level. If we were to fly in formation we were told in which order to take off at this stage, for instance:

"There will be two formations – 'A' Flight will be the port-side formation, led by the Wing Commander and 'B' Flight will be on the starboard, led by myself. Each formation will have four vics of three. Rendezvous will be over Brighton at 10,000 feet, time 1100 hrs. After crossing the coast you will meet the fighters at 1130 hrs."

We were then given the order in which we would be flying, the pilots with the most experience being selected to lead the vics. On every squadron flying experience was the criterion upon which pilots were chosen to lead a formation and at times I, as a humble sergeant, was called upon to lead with a Wing Commander (for instance, one who was a newcomer to the squadron and to wartime flying operations) behind me, proving that the RAF was not rank-conscious in the air.

At the briefing we would naturally pay greatest attention when given our targets and also to the time and place of our rendezvous with the fighters. Concerning the latter set of instructions we had to be as accurate as possible because fighters had not enough petrol to spare for mistakes made by us bomber crews.

An intelligence officer was always present at briefings to tell us what to expect in the way of flak concentrations and enemy fighters and, as he was usually a chap who had done a previous tour of ops himself, he knew the sort of things to warn us about. Each briefing was also attended by a Met Officer, who, with information gleaned from our reconnaissance or weather planes, could give us an idea of what meteorological conditions to expect on the way to, from and over our targets. Needless to say, he had to be good at guessing, as weather forecasting in those days was none too accurate. I clearly remember being told to fly round thunderstorms, if possible, and that if there was one over our target to: "Go and fly over the Zuider Zee for half an hour and hopefully on your return it will have moved on."

Following the briefing, we would get togged-up in flying gear, emptying our pockets of any cash or printed matter such as letters which could have the squadron address on them. However, we were allowed to hang on to our cigarettes, which was a great relief as most of us smoked. Using a checklist we made sure that we had such items as our whistles (with which to draw attention should we ditch into the sea), our 'escape kits' (in case of having to land in enemy territory), plus the appropriate foreign currency, of course.

When preparing for an Op some airman would perform rituals such as always putting on the left boot before the right, for instance, or upon walking out to their planes, several crews would keep to a certain order, such as the navigator leading the pilot and wireless operator. My own personal ritual was only to light up a cigarette when we crossed back over the English coast upon our return journey (while others had begun smoking on their way out on a bombing raid).

Next came an air test on our Blenheim, which had been kept in good shape by always having the same ground crew to look after it. The advantage of this arrangement was that they knew of all its quirks, so consequently played a major role in keeping us safely airborne. In rank we were senior to the three ground crew and did not mix of them socially, but we were all on excellent terms.

For the air test I would meet up with Bill (my Wireless Operator/Air Gunner) and Frank (my Navigator/Bomb Aimer) when Frank would inform Bill of our target. Once in the cockpit I would make sure that everything was working, e.g. that the undercarriage and wing flaps went up and down properly, that the intercom was loud and clear, and that the engine temperature was correct. We usually did one circuit and landing, which also gave Bill a chance to test his radio and fire his guns, while Frank, although he had nothing to test, had his uses as a navigator, with maps which could be employed if the weather suddenly closed in. That situation did occur on our air test once, when we had flown without Frank and visibility suddenly plunged to zero, resulting in us having to fly north until we found an airfield which was clear for us to land, from where we later returned to base.

I must admit to never having asked Frank if he could have flown our kite in an emergency but I was sure that he would have had a jolly good try and could probably have brought it down safely. I made this assumption purely on the fact that we had sat together during many flying hours, when he had observed my every action.

Following the air test, and depending on what time the op was scheduled for, all air crews would assemble in the crew room, where we would pass the time in reading, playing cards and drinking cups of tea or coffee until take-off. With regard to the latter, any extra consumption of tea or coffee never worried us, as we were provided with a bottle in the plane, although I never remember having to use it myself.

Being wartime our Blenheims were usually dispersed around the airfield for safety, so that they could not all be an easy target for intruders, therefore if departure was planned for 0900 hours buses would arrive from 0800 onwards to take us to dispersal, where the groundcrews waited beside their particular aircraft. A couple of footholds in the fuselage enabled Frank, Bill and I to climb up onto the wing, from where we heaved ourselves into the cockpit, closing the sliding roof, which locked from the inside, while Bill headed to the rear.

Upon starting the engine an important job for me was to set the gyroscopic compass, after consulting our ordinary magnetic one. The latter was hard to see, but the trouble with the clearer, gyroscopic compass was that if one became involved in any violent manoeuvres, or if one was to fly in very rough weather, the giro would 'spin', coming to rest in a totally wrong direction. This phenomenon resulted in several of our new crews becoming lost on their return journeys if they had not noticed that their giro had spun. If they were lucky they would be picked up by our ground defence radar as they headed out over the Irish Sea, whereupon a fighter would be sent up to guide them swiftly home. With this in mind I always asked Frank to keep checking that our giro was constantly on the same reading as our magnetic compass.

By the time I had completed all my checks, the ground crew had taken the chocs away and were ready to signal for us to move out. They did this with a cheery 'thumbs-up' sign, and no doubt a fervent prayer that they would soon be reunited with that particular aeroplane on its return safe and sound. From the cockpit I would watch them with a wry smile, wondering if their affectionate concern for our Blenheim included its crew!

The final phase of any operation was the debriefing, when we all went into a room where an intelligence officer, seated behind a desk, solemnly interrogated us in great detail as to how the operation had gone according to each individual aircrew member. The pilot, navigator and air gunner were called in together at first, but if something interesting had happened the officer questioned us separately, so that he could get each man's individual version of events. In spite of feeling cold, hungry, tired and wanting to get the debriefing over with as quickly as possible, we always provided as much detail as we could, although our language on those occasions tended to be more than normally 'colourful', especially if we had been caught up in a lot of enemy flak. During the interview, any claims we made, such as sinking a ship with our bombs, had always to be corroborated by either photographic evidence (provided automatically when bombs were dropped or by our air gunner as we were leaving the target) or by another crew who had been out on the same bombing mission.

One of the perks of having been out on ops was that whatever time of day we returned we were always given our favourite meal, which was bacon and eggs. This was definitely everyone's greatest treat, but due to rationing one had to have been involved directly in thwarting the enemy in order to qualify. Thus a common remark between aircrews walking to their planes was "If I don't return, you may have my bacon and eggs!" Sadly, many did not get back, but the rest of us never received double helpings, of course. It sounds pretty callous nowadays, but as far as missing airmen were concerned, the empty chairs in the mess were both studiously and steadfastly ignored by we, the lucky ones, who no doubt were all secretly thinking, "But for the grace of God I could have bought it too."

Following ops we would usually spend the evening at our local pub, to be met by civilians who always seemed to know where we had been and how many casualties were sustained – something which has puzzled me to this day.

Lack of jealousy between the services

Upon looking back I sometimes dwell on another strange phenomenon, which was that we in our different branches of the armed forces never felt envious of each other – for example, when we met up with the Army, they would say "You poor bloody RAF... We would not have your job", to which we would retort "P.B.I.!" meaning 'poor bloody infantry'. Those in the Navy, including submarine crews, said they admired both the army and the air force but definitely preferred their own service, whatever the duties. But ask any of us chaps in the former services if we wanted to sail the seas and we would have replied "Never!"

It was interesting to note also, how public opinion kept swinging between the Armed Forces: when Germany invaded France our fellow countrymen indignantly demanded. "And where were our infantry?" while when the *Scharnhorst* and *Gneisenau* managed to sneak out of hiding they asked us in the RAF, "And what were *you* doing?"

No doubt the great British public never realised we had been out at the crack of dawn for weeks searching for those two German ships.

While on the subject of not knowing the full story, I will mention here that on the squadron we were all fervent admirers of Winston Churchill, and when he put Air Marshal 'Bomber' Harris in charge of Bomber Command we soon realised that here was a man who could bring about Germany's ultimate defeat. We were proud to be serving under such a dynamic and determined leader but there was a price to pay for Harris's strategy, which was to get every available bomber into the air and out on Ops, whatever the cost. On our squadron alone, for example, casualties sustained due to going out in weather that was totally unfit for flying certainly matched those resulting from enemy action. I am sure that our civilian population at the time was quite ignorant that the 'price' was of so many extra lives being sacrificed by their 'boys in blue' – but perhaps that was just as well – at the end of the day, the expression "the end justifies the means" does tend to spring to mind.

Gordon Shackleton, 2005

Joining Up

Early in 1940 I was told to report to RAF Uxbridge for an interview as a first step towards fulfilling my ambition to become a pilot. After that came a fairly stringent medical exam, the hardest part of which I found was to blow into a U-shaped tube containing mercury for 60 seconds and to hold it at a certain level. For me, the most difficult part was keeping the mouthpiece secure, but I succeeded on my third (and last allowable) attempt.

I was then interviewed by a panel of senior officers, whose function was to decide whether or not I should train as a pilot and if I was "officer material". At the end of the interview I was accepted to take a pilot's course. I was not told, but they obviously decided that this ex-grammar school boy with a London accent would be unlikely to merge into an officers' mess and as a result, at the end of my training I became a sergeant pilot.

On 17th July, my 20th birthday, I received a rail warrant and instructions to report to Number One Receiving Wing, RAF Babbacombe, near Torquay... There were about 20 others on the 9:10am train from Paddington and on arrival at Torquay we were shepherded into columns and herded up to Babbacombe, about 3 miles away – "up" being the operative word. It was uphill all the way and heaving a suitcase on a very warm day was not my idea of fun.

Our introductory week was spent in collecting our uniforms and flying kit, doing some very basic drill and physical training, plus lectures. Included in the flying kit were long-sleeved vests and pants with legs, which I never wore, but which were much appreciated by my father.

Vaccinations were quite an eye-opener; they were all given in the right arm, so as a left-handed writer I was ordered to sit at the table at the head of the line to tick off the names on the list. I was surprised at the number who fainted at the sight of the needle – mostly the biggest and toughest-looking. Injections have never bothered me, but one of my roommates had a violent reaction, became delirious during the night and was taken to hospital by ambulance, never to be seen again by our group...

Initial Training Wing

After two weeks of drill and lectures (the lectures being mainly on the dangers of VD and how to avoid it) we were paraded and marched down to Number Three Initial Training Wing in the middle of Torquay for six weeks of misery...

In Torquay we were billeted in a row of old bed-and-breakfast-type hotels overlooking the harbour. When the hotels were commandeered, everything movable was taken out, to be replaced with iron bedsteads and lockers. Our mess was the corner building, where we gathered three times a day for boring, tasteless meals in which liver and mince played a major role. For three consecutive days we had mince at each mealtime and in the early hours of the fourth day I woke with severe stomach pains.

On staggering from my room I discovered that both stairs and landing were covered with bodies doubled up in agony. At 7am, when the orderly Sergeant made his usual rounds to inquire who wished to report sick, all five in our room requested to see the medical officer. He returned later to order us out on parade, as apparently the "powers that be" had decided that 200 airmen missing (i.e. the whole group) was unacceptable. Fortunately, that morning we had lectures, so by the afternoon we had recovered sufficiently to manage drill and PT. The MO, we heard later, went berserk when he heard we had not been allowed to see him. However, as a result the kitchen was fumigated and cleaned and our diet did improve somewhat...

At this point I will add that the only item of food I dislike is liver, but being constantly ravenous due to our intensive training, I would nevertheless devour the lot – smothered in sauce to disguise the taste.

Our days began with inspection parade at 8am, followed by drill and PT in the morning and in the afternoons, lectures on airmanship, navigation and Morse code. Our daily chores took place at the harbour, where our drill sergeant stood on the very edge of the quay, happily oblivious to the fact that 200 minds were willing him to step backwards into the drink … but no such luck!

In the unlikely event that one's buttons and boots had passed his inspection, one's hair became the focus of attention. I found myself having to make twice-weekly trips to the barber, whose usual charge was one shilling, but having nothing to cut, I was charged threepence for putting a razor to my neck.

One night I was detailed for guard duty outside the billet, with instructions to challenge anyone after 11pm and inspect their identity card. I only challenged one person, who fortunately was a friend and not a foe. As I had no weapon or torch, I had to humble myself by asking him for a match to check his card.[1]

At the end of six weeks I emerged so slim and fit I could have joined a Guards regiment as a drill instructor, but instead I was posted to Elementary Flying Training School at RAF Carlisle. I was soon to appreciate the difference in climate between the North and South of England. I left Torquay in a heatwave at 4 pm and arrived at Carlisle at 6 am the next morning to be greeted by icy blasts which had caused recent rain puddles to freeze solid!

---

[1] It was obvious that sentry duty was never meant to be my forte. Whilst in the Home Guard, awaiting call-up, I had a similar embarrassing experience (see page 129).

Flying Solo

From Carlisle station we were taken to Kingsdown airfield, which had been used by a pre-war flying club and where the RAF had provided some Nissen huts for our lecture rooms and mess. All personnel were billeted in private homes on the bus route to the city and the house where I stayed was so cold that I used to wear my padded inner flying suit in bed. My landlady was rather dour but she did allow me to use her iron one evening, even offering to show me how to iron shirts. Naturally, I hoped she would finish my ironing, but no such luck! Having worked in a laundry before marriage, she demonstrated how to fold a shirt exactly as if it was new … an accomplishment which I retain to this day.

Upon arrival we were briefed as to our duties, namely on alternate days we would fly in the morning with lectures in the afternoon and vice-versa.

I was posted to 'A' Flight, my instructor being a sergeant who not once during the six-week course gave me a word of encouragement, just biting criticism and was so spiteful that out of six pupils assigned to him, three asked to be taken off the course.

The flying instructors were all RAF personnel and the lecturers all civilians; the one teaching airmanship ensuring our success in passing the final examination by displaying the answers on the blackboard!

From 'A' Flight, situated on the perimeter of the airfield, we would watch in awe as 'B' Flight instructors took off in a formation, flew round in a tight 'V' and broke off with a "Prince of Wales feathers". We were told that 'B' Flight instructors did this every morning before getting down to the serious business of teaching.

Our aeroplanes were not the usual Tiger Moths, which most learners flew, but Miles Magisters – monoplanes which had the reputation of being unreliable in a spin. If an aircraft loses flying speed, it stalls, and then if the wing drops it goes into a spin. This is normally corrected by putting the joystick forward, building up flying speed and then applying the opposite rudder. However, we were warned that if a Magister were to go into a spin there was no guarantee that the plane would respond...

The maximum time allowed for a learner to "solo" was 12 hours. I made my first solo flight in ten, but in common with most pupils I found it incredibly difficult to master the art of keeping the wings even whilst at the same time maintaining level flight. It suddenly all "clicked", however, rather like riding a bicycle for the first time.

We pupils referred to practise landings as "circuits and bumps", when, having taken off and circled the aerodrome, we would try to return to earth smoothly.

"You chaps always land your kites about six times," an instructor observed one day. "You can't manage to get down and stay down, so it's bump, bump, bump!"

On our third morning in the 'A' Flight position we heard 'B' Flight start up their engines on the far side of the airfield and saw three machines in V formation heading towards us, still on the ground but getting steadily nearer. The leader in the centre was aiming straight for us, and at the very last minute the pilot lowered his flaps and the plane leapt into the air, its wheels bouncing on our roof and clearing it by inches. It landed on a house, fortunately unoccupied, by the main road opposite, the plane's occupants escaping unhurt, but the Magister on the left never did get off the ground, demolishing the ground defence tent and killing a soldier inside it, while the third plane crashed into the perimeter fence.

We learned that hoarfrost on the wings, which interrupted the airflow, was the cause of the accident. The Air Ministry issued an order, to take immediate effect, that frost must be removed before take-off. Needless to say such an initiation was not exactly a confidence-booster for us budding aviators...

Landing on Clouds

Early in pilot training, landings were a difficult procedure to master. Magisters and Tiger Moths had landing speeds varying from 60 to 70 miles per hour, increasing with high-speed aircraft to over 150 miles per hour.

The earlier planes had an old-fashioned type of landing gear – two wheels at the front and two at the back – but also being introduced were the latest types of undercarriages, so different skills had to be learned and mastered.

Instead of levelling off a few feet above the airstrip, throttling back and letting the plane stall and sail down gently into a three-point landing, the aim was to fly near to the ground, letting the wheels touch down and then closing the throttles.

Until this new technique was mastered, undercarriages were being written off on a regular basis, many of them being left embedded in the earth if it was soft.

In order to prevent this, I and other pilots on the squadron used to practise 'landing' on cirrus clouds, which were flat-topped as opposed to the fluffy cumulus variety. These practise landings were approved, provided that the cloud-base was above 2,000 feet, which allowed flying speed to build up so that we would not stall and fall out of the sky.

It would have been embarrassing trying to explain later that the reason for a crash had been due to "landing on the cloud"!

Near Crashes

Most piston-engined planes had a tendency to 'swing' on take-off, this being due to torque, and in order to combat this, the pilot would apply the opposite rudder to keep a straight course, although when landing the swing was not so pronounced. On one of my early solo flights I was so pleased at having made a perfect 'three-point touchdown' that I forgot to correct the swing and to my horror discovered that I was racing towards a line of parked planes. Frantically applying the opposite rudder made no difference, so seconds before an inevitable collision I pulled on the emergency brake, applied full rudder and by pure chance stopped perfectly in line with the other parked machines. Fully expecting a reprimand, I was surprised and relieved that my carelessness went unnoticed...

The next day I was chatting to an airman who revealed that he was in Flying Control and complained of the reckless antics of some of the instructors. As an example he cited the crazy behaviour of one the day before, who on landing had charged towards a line of parked aircraft, only at the very last minute sliding into place. Not surprisingly I remained silent...

In the last days of the course my instructor said that having had no time to practise aerobatics together I could go up on my own, saying: "climb to 5,000 feet, try looping the loop and then if you are happy, do some slow rolls."

After I had successfully looped I followed with a slow roll. However, having turned completely over, all the dust from the floor was deposited all over me and some of it got under my goggles, blinding me.

On opening my eyes I discovered that I was flying upside down in complete silence.[2]

Having moved the stick both ways without any change in position I had visions of either landing upside down or baling out.

I had really given up hope of righting the plane when in sheer desperation I pulled the joystick towards me and came out safely.

---

[2] One of the Magister's quirks, which I did not know then, was that the engine would stop when inverted, due to the carburettor being gravity-fed. Fortunately, on being returned to normal flying attitude the engine would restart of its own accord.

Cranfield

On completion of the course I was awarded an "above average" rating and posted to No. 14 Flying Training School at Cranfield, to train on twin-engined Oxfords.

My posting to Cranfield and Oxfords was somewhat of a disappointment; I would much rather have trained on single-engined planes, preferably Spitfires, prior to being posted to a fighter squadron (fancying myself as a Douglas Bader in the making!).

Cranfield was a pre-war, all-grass airfield with modern, comfortable facilities and the pattern of training was similar to Carlisle; lectures in the morning and flying for the rest of the day. My flying instructor was a pleasant, friendly and encouraging sergeant who, after only five hours 'dual', sent me off for my first solo flight in an Oxford.

Forced Landings

Soon afterwards he decided to teach me how to do a 'precautionary landing' in a restricted space with full control of the aircraft. For normal landings on an aerodrome the approach was made at an angle of roughly 45 degrees, crossing the airfield boundary at 40 to 50 feet up with an airspeed approximately 15 miles per hour above stalling, which allows for a margin of error if for any reason the landing has to be aborted. However, if the landing has to be made in a small field the technique is totally different, for then the object is to touch down as near to the perimeter as possible, approaching at a flat angle, just above stalling speed, and crossing the boundary very low, cutting the power and applying the brakes at the moment of touchdown.

As we descended I began putting my instructor's teaching into practice, keeping the flaps fully extended, with only the power of the engines keeping our Oxford in the air, the plane's attitude, nose-up and tail down, being most important because then I could later apply the brakes without fear of somersaulting.

On that fateful day we were 50 feet up and 50 yards from landing and I was preparing to close the throttles ready to sink gently to the ground when our port engine failed...

Immediately I applied maximum power to the starboard engine but with no effect. The port wing dropped suddenly and we dived towards a Blenheim which was preparing to take off and hit it broadside on. Just before I assumed the crash position I was relieved to see three airmen running from the stationary plane. The noise on impact was horrendous, followed by dead silence, except for the dripping sound of petrol escaping from the ruptured tanks, something which inspired me and my instructor to bail out quickly in case of fire. Having slid down the wing I discovered my left leg was unable to bear my weight, but it's amazing how fast one can crawl when threatened with an explosion...

Fortunately, apart from some minor cuts to his face my instructor was proclaimed fit, but I was not so lucky. Upon medical examination my left leg was found to be badly injured and the heel smashed, requiring stitches. Our M.O. also mentioned that my spinal x-ray showed some damage. However, after spending three days in sick bay, which was overflowing, I was offered seven days sick leave provided I vacated my bed immediately, which I gratefully did.

Before arriving home I phoned my mother to say that I had fallen down stairs in the blackout and not be too shocked by my appearance. I myself had been staggered when I saw my face for the first time following the incident; I looked as if I had lost an argument with a mincing machine!

Some years later I began having back problems and an x-ray revealed an old injury to my spine which could only have been caused by the plane crash.

On a later occasion, when I was an instructor, one of my pupils landed in a field away from base but phoned to say that the plane was undamaged. With another instructor I was ordered to fetch it back. As we circled above the abandoned plane I said to my colleague "That field looks a bit small..."

"Nonsense!" came the reply. "If a pupil can land without damage, then surely we can too."

I made a textbook precautionary landing, braking immediately the wheels touched, but we still finished up in the far hedge, fortunately without any damage to the aircraft.

That evening we asked the pupil how he managed to land in such a confined space and could not help but roar with laughter at his reply:

"I cheated rather," he explained, "I actually landed in the next field but I bounced over the hedge!"

Lighthearted interludes such as the above were invaluable in counteracting stressful events, although in those times we were all young and resilient, so a few days home leave would work magic.

After crashing into the Blenheim I arrived back at base a week later to be met by my instructor carrying his blood-stained parachute and we were off again...

Too Close For Comfort

Later there is an account of when Frank, Bill and I were peppered with very accurate flak. All aircrews were equipped with tin hats to wear over their flying helmets when in enemy territory, but most of us had priorities other than our heads so used to sit on the metal hats at dangerous moments. On this particular day Frank forgot to take that precaution, however, and his nether regions were therefore unprotected when shrapnel ripped through our aircraft.

After landing we were approached by the ground crew, who were amazed that our battered plane had remained airborne. Upon looking at Frank one of the mechanics asked if it was only the knee of his trousers which had been torn by a piece of shell and smilingly Frank replied "Yes".

"Then how did you get *that* hole?" asked the airman, pointing to Frank's groin, whereupon our brave bomb aimer passed out cold...

Gripped By Fear

When I was more experienced I was ordered to fly a groundstaff fitter to another airfield in an Anson – an obsolete twin-engined plane with manually operated flaps, which had to be pumped down by the pilot. We were on the final approach so I reached behind to pump down the flaps.

On completion of this task I resumed my normal sitting position for the actual touchdown, only to find my passenger had grabbed the dual control column and in spite of my requests would not let go.

He was frozen with fear and I had to batter him with my fists before he succumbed.

After landing safely I asked him what the hell he had been doing.

"I thought you had lost control," he replied, somewhat sheepishly "and that I had better take over"!

Lectures

Lectures were varied and intense and included navigation, which meant that the private tuition I had received in trigonometry prior to my call-up proved invaluable but the calculus I had studied was never used.

We spent hours learning the Morse Code plus more time sending and receiving while we also learned how to operate the radio telephone (or R.T.).

Meteorology had a soporific effect on me, so I had great difficulty in staying awake, possibly because while slides were being shown the room was in semi-darkness.

Outranked at a Dorchester 'Do'

Our advanced flying training now included cross-country navigation with map-reading, plus plotting courses while taking wind speeds and direction into consideration. 'Link training' was also part of the course; a tedious but effective way of practising how to rely only on instruments. It involved being shut into a large box and receiving instructions via headphones of compass headings by which to steer – a far cry from the sophisticated flight simulators used to train airline pilots today.

Once I was competent to fly and land on one engine and had mastered formation flying, which demanded total concentration, I was ready to move onto night flying, which was quite scary at first, as the instructor failed to warn me that at night when the throttles are opened for take off a sheet of flame, invisible in daylight, engulfs both sides of the fuselage.

Having successfully map-read and navigated ten cross-countrys of approximately two hours duration I was paired with another trainee called Mason in February 1941. He piloted the first leg of a cross-country while I navigated, then upon arriving back at base we changed over. After roughly two more hours the weather began to deteriorate; visibility was poor, the cloud base was down to 1,000 feet and it began to snow. I spotted a barrage balloon in the distance, so I inquired of Mason, now navigating, where we were.

"Somewhere near Bedford?" came his uncertain reply.

Since I knew there were no barrage balloons over Bedford I guessed we must have been approaching London. With less than an hour of daylight left, snow falling and totally lost, I decided that a precautionary landing was required.

I spied a field without any obstacles, which seemed okay, and made a good touchdown, stopping a few yards from the boundary fence. I cut the engines and opened the door in the side of the fuselage to see some Home Guard chaps charging towards us with fixed bayonets. I swiftly closed the door and waited for them to knock!

In due course an RAF team, headed by an officer, arrived from Uxbridge to mount a guard over the plane. The officer informed us that we were at Kings Langley, near a London Underground station, and that nobody would be any the wiser if we stayed the night in Town. Mason helpfully volunteered the information that he lived at Hyde Park, so we could spend the night at his house.

On the Tube train we caused quite a stir in our battledress and flying boots, carrying parachutes, resulting in whispered speculation that we were shot-down fighter pilots returning to base.

On arrival at his Hyde Park home, Mason rang the bell and the door was opened by young lady wearing a long evening gown, who turned out to be his sister.

"Gully darling! How lovely to see you! We are just off to the Dorchester for Granddaddy's birthday party, so you must come and bring your friend," she gushed, happily.

Thus, much against my better judgement, we arrived at the Dorchester by taxi and were directed to the grand ballroom. To my horror the place was bristling with senior officers from all three services, including generals, admirals and air marshals. I only saw two lower ranks during the entire evening, who were corporals. However, both were sporting monocles so in civilian life were obviously totally eligible in 'Society'.

Notwithstanding, we were made very welcome by our birthday host (who was a Lord and chairman of the Midland Bank) plus Mason's father, who was, at the time, the MP for Croydon.

Needless to say I was so overwhelmed by being at such a "posh do", amongst so many top brass, whilst wearing only my trainee pilot's battledress (we were both only leading aircraftmen, equivalent to Army Lance corporals) that I stayed in the background all evening and alas cannot recall that delicious Dorchester birthday repast.

Nevertheless, it was an interesting experience to look back on and one which proved that all those precautionary landings I had practised had paid off in the end.

Meeting My Crew at OTU

On 17th May 1941, now the proud possessor of a pair of pilot's wings on my left breast pocket, three sergeant's stripes on my sleeves and an 'above average' rating as a pilot, I was posted to No.17 Operational Training Unit (OTU) at RAF Upwood in Lincolnshire.

Upon arrival I was introduced to the crew with whom I would share all future operational duties. My navigator/bomb aimer was Sergeant Frank Eyres, who hailed from Southport, though much to his chagrin was always introduced as "from near Blackpool". My wireless operator/air gunner was Sergeant Bill Kennedy, a native of Stirling in Scotland who, we discovered, became almost totally incomprehensible when overexcited, such as when we were attacked by the German Messerschmitt 109 fighters...

For our last exercise at OTU we had to complete a cross-country carrying four high explosive bombs to be dropped on a seaside bombing range. Unfortunately, Bill chose that day to oversleep, so we were two hours late in setting off. The meteorological report had forecast deteriorating weather conditions and for the second half of the trip we were in low cloud, flying on instruments. By the time we found the bombing range we were below cloud at 500 feet, but as 800 feet was the minimum height considered safe to drop bombs unless they were the delayed-action type, we elected not to jettison them.

By the time we were approaching base we had descended down to 300 feet and I made the decision not to land with bombs on board. We dropped them 'safe' in a field, but unfortunately the incendiaries ignited on impact. Upon landing I was congratulated by a worried chief flying instructor, who, however, was not too pleased upon hearing later that we had set fire to a farmer's field of wheat.

In spite of our various hiccups we had, by the end of our intensive eight-week course, learned to work as a team, having mastered close formation flying, three-hour cross countrys by day and night, low and high-level bombing, plus air-to-ground firing at targets.

Bill became expert at obtaining wireless fixes for navigational aids, while Frank too was proficient at navigating by dead reckoning. At the end of the course, as a crew, we were rated 'above average'.

The aircraft we had learned to master was a Bristol Blenheim, although upon completion of our training we could be posted to operational squadrons flying American Boston's, de Havilland Mosquitos or Blenheim Mk IVs. The Bostons had a crew of three, a speed in excess of 280 miles an hour, were fitted with cannons firing forward and backward plus a bomb load of 2,500lbs.

Mosquitos, on the other hand, had a crew of two, a speed of over 350 miles per hour, and eight machine guns or four cannons firing forward.[3] In 1941 the Mossie's bomb load was about 2,500lbs, but by 1942/3 they were able to carry 'blockbusters' weighing 4,000lbs.

The third option was to be sent to Blenheim Squadron. These planes had a crew of three, a bomb load of 1,000lbs, twin machine guns in a rear turret and one forward-firing gun, which was pilot-operated. Their maximum speed was just 266 miles per hour, yet they were still operating in daylight at low levels and thus suffered horrendous losses.

Joining such a squadron would be stepping into dead men's shoes – an official Air Ministry document published after the war revealed that in 1940/1 the average life of an operational Blenheim crew was just 5½ hours in the air.

It was to one of the latter that Frank, Bill and I were posted...

---

[3] At that time, rear-firing guns were regarded as unnecessary, as there were no German fighters able to match the speed of the Mosquito.

Posted to a Blenheim Squadron

When we arrived at 114 Squadron, one of the last still operating with Blenheims, at West Raynham in Norfolk, we discovered that with two other crews from Upwood we made up a total of only six crews – although before losses 18 crews had been normal squadron strength.

Our first sight of West Raynham airfield was of four prewar hangars which had been badly damaged by the bombs of German hit-and-run raiders the previous day. The 114 Squadron flying crews had been hastily evacuated to Weasenham Hall, three miles from the aerodrome. A beautiful 18th century mansion, Weasenham Hall belonged to a charming family who had been allowed to stay on, albeit in the servants quarters, while the main building was taken over by the RAF. Still, as they said, this was just one of the many upheavals resulting from the war.

Any ideas we may have had about being eased gently into life on an operational squadron were immediately dispelled upon our arrival, as during our first week we were in the air for nearly 50 hours, practising close formation flying, which was hard both physically and mentally, but good preparation for what was to come.

During 1940 our fighters had been very successful against the German Messerschmitt 109s, downing them at a rate of two to one, but by 1941 there were not enough enemy bombers or fighters raiding England by day, so we had to start fighter sweeps to catch them over France. However, it was soon discovered that unless bombers were included, the Germans stayed on the ground, and so the 'circus' was born. This was a handful of bombers, usually Blenheims, with a very large fighter escort, sent to bomb targets at heights varying from 10,000 to 20,000 feet, which had to be within the escorts' range.

A 'Circus' to Lille

My first operation from West Raynham was a 'circus' to Lille at 14,000 feet with an escort of Spitfires and Hurricanes surrounding us above and below.

Apart from puffs of innocent-looking black smoke, which we soon discovered was deadly flak, we saw nothing, but the fighters seemed happy with their result; we had been the bait and apparently it had worked.

Our next circus was nearly a disaster, as some bright spark at Group Headquarters had decided that if heavy flak was most effective from between 10 and 20 thousand feet and light flak was best up to 6,000 feet, if we went in at 8,000 feet we should be between the two.

In actual fact we got the full brunt of both kinds of flak and all took a terrible pounding, arriving back somewhat the worse for wear. No one was actually shot down, but the damage in terms of holes in fuselages was quite extensive.

Attacking German Convoys

By the third week in September we had acquired reinforcements as another six crews arrived from OTU and in addition to circuses 2 Group, to which we belonged, was assigned to attack German shipping in the North Sea.

Their merchant ships moved in convoys, heavily escorted by flak ships and destroyers. Our reconnaissance planes would report a convoy in a certain area and then up to a dozen bombers, usually Blenheims, would be dispatched, loaded with 11-second delayed-action bombs to attack at low level (i.e. wave height).

The large formation would split up about 20 miles from the enemy coast and approach in 'vics' of three, approximately six miles apart, turning parallel to the coast and flying at three miles a minute for three minutes, thus the 12 planes would be able to spot a convoy anywhere in a 60 square-mile area.

Our losses at that time were horrendous, because, apart from being shot down by anti-aircraft fire, as soon as our planes were sighted, Messerschmitt 109s would stream out from their European bases at twice our speed and chase us home. However, the BBC Evening News at that time would report something like: *"RAF bombers attacked German shipping in the North Sea today and six of our aircraft are missing."* What they failed to mention was that they were six out of only a possible 12 – i.e. 50 percent losses!

On one occasion we were sent to patrol along the Dutch coast with 11 other Blenheims; we sighted nothing but, sadly, three failed to return.

On 15th September we were ordered to attack a German convoy off the Friesian Islands. Having crossed the North Sea we ran into a blinding rainstorm and as we emerged we were greeted by what appeared to be a wall of tracer bullets coming from a flak ship escorting the convoy. To my utter amazement and intense relief what had appeared as a solid wall of bullets, all coming straight for us, deflected at the last moment before impact, but for the first time in my life I had been convinced that I was going to die.

Then, suddenly, in front of us loomed an enemy ship of about 3,000 tons, positioned broadside-on. We stormed in at sea-level and Frank released our two 500-pound delayed-action bombs[4] just seconds before we climbed over the mast and dived down the other side between two lines of ships.

---

[4] Perhaps an explanation is required here; attacking a ship at deck level using 11-second delayed-action bombs at the velocity of 200 miles per hour has the same effect as a torpedo entering her hull.

We then 'ran the gauntlet' for some three miles before emerging, only to be attacked by a Messerschmitt 109.

By the time he disengaged, Bill was able to report a large explosion on the ship we had attacked.

Unfortunately, our bomb-release camera had taken a photo just as we turned for home and only succeeded in filming our rudder, so we were only allowed to claim a 'probable' hit, for without photographic evidence claiming a sinking was not allowed.

More Circuses

From the middle of September until the end of the month we did three more circuses, including two to Mazingarbe, the first at 12,000 feet, a second at 14,000 feet, while the third was to Cherbourg, where two large ships were in the docks.

On each occasion the operations were successful in bringing up the German fighters, which was really the object of the exercise, and fortunately for us they were not able to penetrate our defensive screen of fighter aircraft.

The flak was heaviest over Cherbourg, but apart from a few holes in the fuselage we suffered little damage.

During October we were kept quite busy on Army cooperation exercises, then on the 13th we were once again sent on a circus to Mazingarbe at 14,000 feet. However, this was our third visit in a month and Jerry had obviously anticipated our return, reinforcing his defences accordingly.

As a result we were subjected to heavy flak all the way from the coast to the target and back again, with some casualties.

Low-Level Shipping Beats

On the 15th we were once again on low-level shipping beats off Norway when our formation of three attacked a large convoy defended by several flak ships and destroyers. We attacked a ship of about 4,000 tons (which was later confirmed as sunk) and in spite of heavy tracers from all sides we returned safely.

At the end of the month we were briefed to attack the aerodrome at Lannion in north-west France on the Atlantic coast, so we landed at Redruth in Cornwall to refuel and pick up a fighter escort. As a result of the attack runways were confirmed as having been severely damaged and we suffered no losses during over six hours of formation flying, which pleased the Air Ministry.

The November weather was particularly bad for operational purposes and the powers-that-be had obviously decided that the old Blenheim was too vulnerable for daylight sorties and switched us to night-intruding raids.

The Germans, meanwhile, were using heavy bombers for mine-laying in the Thames and Humber, operating from large airfields in Holland which were outside the range of our night fighters.

The minelaying aircraft would radio their base when they had laid their mines, but their signals were intercepted by our intelligence services. Our job was to patrol over the Dutch airfields, keeping them shut down for several hours so the German bombers were eventually diverted to French aerodromes, where our night fighters could attack them as they landed.

Shutting Down Herdla

Having spent a large part of November perfecting our night-flying skills it came as no surprise that following a night raid to Ostend docks early in December we were then told to start practising daylight bombing again at various levels from 50 feet upwards!

We did not know at the time but the object of the exercise was to discover the minimum height at which bombs would stick into concrete and not bounce. This proved to be 300 feet, but nobody in their right mind other than kamikaze pilots would ever contemplate bombing from that height!

For three days on the 19th, 20th and 21st we stood by from dawn until dusk, waiting for a break in the weather, then at lunchtime on the 22nd we were able to take off, bound for RAF Lossiemouth in Scotland...

Upon arrival we were put on 'security blackout' and ordered not to make phone calls or write any letters, the whole of 114 Squadron, including ground crews, being confined to base. One of our concerns, I recall, was the effect that this would have on our families so close to Christmas.

The general opinion was that something 'very hush-hush' was in the offing for the next day, especially when we were told to be in bed by 9.30pm and to abstain from alcohol, but at 9pm as we were soberly making our way to bed, we were informed that the operation was postponed for 24 hours, a situation which was repeated on a daily basis, with the result that for the whole of the festive season we were in limbo until the morning of the 27th, when we were finally briefed for an operation.

We were to be part of a combined operation on Norway, Vaagso being the target of the main force. Our Squadron was ordered to shut down a fighter aerodrome at Herdla for 24 hours, destroying the y-shaped runways, which demanded very accurate bombing from 300 feet. Before leaving we had been told to be prepared for 50 percent losses, so anyone surviving could expect a 'gong'.

Twelve Blenheims plus two reserves took off and formed one large V formation for the three-hour flight across the North Sea, led by our Wing Commander and the Squadron navigation officer, who kept us below enemy radar beams but ready at the last moment to pull up to bombing level after crossing the Norwegian coast.

Suddenly a white, wintry landscape came into view, looking so beautiful I almost forgot to be scared, especially as we roared in at zero feet with the local population all emerging from their little snow-covered houses to give us a wave! Much to our amazement and relief we encountered no flak until we had crossed and bombed the runways, on which Messerschmitt 109 fighters were in the throes of take-off.

Having dropped their bombs, our planes made a left turn for home, but unfortunately the two reserves on the inside of the formation were unable to slow down sufficiently with the result that their wings touched and they both crashed, lack of height and airspace being the cause. It was extraordinarily unlucky, especially in view of the fact that the reserve aircraft had made the entire trip instead of returning immediately to base when not required.

All the Blenheims carried backward-firing cameras which operated as the bombs were released and when developed the films showed 26 hits on the runways from 52 bombs dropped, plus the Messerschmitt 109s in total confusion, one having been photographed with its tail in the middle of a bomb burst.

It had proved practically impossible to shut down aerodromes with grass runways, because the whole airfield could usually be used in an emergency.[5] However, Herdla aero-

---

[5] Tangmere fighter aerodrome on the south coast was a good example, as I discovered one afternoon when refuelling there, as we often did prior to returning to base after crossing the Channel. That morning it had been bombed by enemy aircraft from 200 feet, yet because there were no

drome was on a rocky island on which railway sleepers had been laid with concrete poured into the gaps, therefore our intense bombing raid closed it for more than 24 hours, and as a consequence the UK's combined force was free from air attack.

Our Wing Commander was awarded a well-deserved DSO and his navigator a bar to his DFC, while, unsurprisingly, the rest of us received nothing...

The following day we flew back to West Raynham, where we were given a 48-hour leave pass – and so ended in an unforgettable Christmas.

---

concrete runways the bomb holes were quickly bulldozed in, leaving it fully operational within hours. I should mention here, of course, that as the war progressed the faster, heavier aircraft needed longer, stronger runways which would be unaffected by the elements such as rain and snow, therefore grass runways were gradually phased out, to be replaced by those made from concrete and tarmac.

The Big Freeze

1942 came in with a bang. In January the weather was really appalling and for the whole month temperatures in Norfolk were sub-zero, the snow being so deep and solid that everyone on the station was ordered out on the airfield to clear it away. The freeze up lasted right through February and into early March.

We were only able to operate on one night in January, the 28th, when we were ordered to intrude on Schipol aerodrome in Holland.

However, as we approached the target our port engine put on a spectacular display of pyrotechnics before stopping, so we were forced to limp home on one engine only.

Confronting the *Scharnhorst* and *Gneisenau*

From the beginning of February we were standing by from dawn until dusk, as was the whole of Bomber Command, waiting for the German battleships *Scharnhorst* and *Gneisenau* to make their breakout from Brest, where they had been having damage repaired. They were expected to make a dash through the English Channel back to their home ports in Germany, with a strong fighter escort, so it was planned that our fighters would engage theirs, allowing our bombers freedom to bomb the ships from 10,000 feet in large formations.

On the 12th of February the weather was atrocious and at lunchtime we were stood down and told to return to our billets. However, 20 minutes following our arrival at Weasenham Hall we were ordered to report back to the operations room, where we were told that the two ships were actually half way up the Channel, having slipped out of Brest harbour unseen, due to the awful weather. We were briefed to climb above the clouds and rendezvous in formation, then, if we were able to find a hole in the clouds, to bomb the targets, otherwise we should descend individually and attack any ships that could be seen.

There were no breaks in the clouds, so we began descending, relying purely on instruments, which, due to the bumpy conditions, were all over the place. I was kept very busy keeping control of the aircraft so I ordered Frank to watch the altimeter and tell me when we were below 1,000 feet, then to keep on calling the height until we broke cloud cover, which we did at 400 feet – immediately over one of the big ships!

Fortunately Frank was too surprised to release the bombs, because at 400 feet we would have been blown to Kingdom Come ourselves had he been foolish enough to do so. We were promptly set upon by two Messerschmitt 109s but within seconds we got safely back up into the freezing clouds. However, after a few minutes, ice began forming on the wings, with chunks of it breaking off and hitting the fuselage, while, to crown it all, the port engine's carburettor froze and stopped. I then had no option but to drop down again, when thankfully the engine restarted. Visibility was only about 400 yards but we were very near to a German destroyer, which promptly opened fire on us, so back into the clouds we went...

By mutual agreement we decided that there was no point in hanging about to be fired at and chased by fighters, when even if we did bomb from 400 to 500 feet, the only damage would most likely be to us. Thankfully, more by luck than good judgement, we eventually found our way back to West

Raynham, with daylight fading and minimal visibility, having dumped our bomb load into the North Sea. During that operation three of our Squadron were lost, mainly due to the terrible weather, combined with the inexperience of the recently-arrived crews.

Bombing Soesterburg Aerodrome

On the 16th of February we were on standby all evening until nearly midnight, when we were briefed to intrude on Soesterburg aerodrome, our orders being to patrol for one hour in the vicinity of the target and to bomb it when and if the flare path lit up. We were told that the Germans had several dummy flare paths dotted around, which could be recognised by their perfect symmetry and also their persistent invitations of green lights to land.

After an hour or so we were over the target and, as it was a clear, moonlit night, Frank had no difficulty in identifying the aerodrome, which was then in darkness. We circled around, keeping watch, ignoring the 'welcome to land' green lights from several dummys, until eventually the real flare path was illuminated, which was our cue to move in and drop half our bombs.

A little while later Soesterburg was open for business again and we successfully dropped the rest of our bombs, but as we did so the port engine packed up. Knowing our relief had arrived, we set course for home, then just before crossing the English coast the engine restarted, so we were able to land normally, thank goodness.

Losing My Cool

On the ground we were guided by an airman rotating two torches until they suddenly went out and we were left impatiently waiting for what seemed an age, freezing and gasping for hot drink.

Then, at last, I spotted a groundcrew man ducking under the port wing, so I pushed back the cockpit cover and slipped down the wing.

As my feet touched the icy ground I fell flat on my back, banging my head. That was the very last straw and in a fury I picked myself up, hurled myself at the groundcrew man and gave him a very graphic description of what it was like flying for three to four hours, being shot at from below and in the air, and coping with a dodgy engine.

Eventually I had to take a breath, which gave him the chance to say how sorry he was for our predicament but that he was actually off-duty and was taking a short-cut from the village.

That was a salutary lesson to me and to this day I have never allowed my temper to run out of control.

A Tricky Air Test

A few days later with a new engine fitted I took our Blenheim 'L' for London for a test flight, only to discover that I had no air speed indicator... I was not unduly bothered, being confident that I could cope as in my mind the only thing which might have been dangerous was if, for some reason, the landing had to be aborted, so I called up control and asked for a 'priority' landing.

After taxiing back to dispersal the reason for the instrument failure became apparent: the fitter had not removed the pitot head cover and thus the pressure of air, which operated the instruments, had been cut off. The poor chap was in a state of shock as a result and I was quite certain he would never make the same mistake again.

Later I was ordered to report to my flight commander, a very large man with an explosive temper, who gave me the biggest dressing-down possible for not putting the fitter on a charge for endangering the aircraft and putting the lives of the crew at risk. My punishment was to wash down two planes, but the next day, when he had calmed down, my Squadron leader (i.e. the flight commander) admitted that I had done well in the crisis.

"A Piece Of Cake"

On the last day of February we were briefed for a circus at 10,000 feet to Ostend docks and as an 'old hand' I was approached by some of the newly-arrived crews and asked what being in a circus was like. I explained that in the six months I had been on the Squadron we had suffered no losses on circuses, which were considered "a piece of cake".

Oh dear! Over the target we ran into a box barrage of very accurate flak. Frank took a piece of shell through a fold in the knee of his trousers, while I was hit in the back by six-inch lump of shrapnel, which first came through a steel petrol-cock before penetrating the back of my seat and lodging in my flying suit.

We limped home, sporting gaping holes in the fuselage and with the starboard engine vibrating like mad, but one of the good things about the old Blenheim was that her radial engines (air cooled) would keep going even when damaged by flak. With our fingers crossed that the engine would hold out we eventually reached base some 20 minutes after the rest of the Squadron, to quite a celebrity welcome, but it was a near escape for poor old 'L' for London, which had suffered so much damage that she was almost beyond repair.

Looping the Loop

By the end of February 1942 No.114 Squadron was the only squadron operating with Mark IV Blenheims, the rest of 2 Group having been reequipped with Bostons, Mosquitos or Mitchells (although the American Mitchells were soon discovered to be unsuitable for 2 Group operations).

The short-nosed Mark I Blenheim came into service in 1937 as a night-fighter, but within a couple of years it became obvious that it was no match for the German fighters, so with the modification of the nose extension it became the Mark IV and was used as a bomber, capable of carrying a 1,000lb bomb load.

At West Raynham we had one short-nosed Blenheim, which was livelier to handle and in a rash moment I agreed to see if it would loop-the-loop...

On a beautiful day early in March and with the whole station watching I took off and climbed to 10,000 feet and then, with the throttle fully opened I pushed the nose down into a near vertical dive...

With the air speed indicator registering 350 miles per hour, everything vibrating like mad, the wings about to come off and 5,000 feet on the clock it required every ounce of strength I had to pull her out of the dive.

Still at full throttle I started the long climb up to the top of the loop, which I finally reached with just 65 miles per hour on the speedometer, a fraction above stalling speed.

Quite an experience!

Mistaken Identity

In addition to the magnetic compass all RAF planes were equipped with gyroscopic compasses which could, if subjected to violent changes in direction or height, spin and then regain their equilibrium, but would then have to be reset using the magnetic compass.

One night, one of our inexperienced pilots was returning from a night operation and failed to notice that his gyroscopic compass had spun after taking violent evasive action; low on fuel and lost he decided on an emergency landing.

As his navigator was not sure if they were in France, Holland or back in England, they awaited first light to reconnoitre the area on foot, whereupon the first thing they saw was a windmill.

Obeying standing orders (i.e. not to allow their aircraft fall into enemy hands) they duly set fire to it...

Only later did they discover that they were in Lincolnshire and not in Holland!

Bird Trouble

For the next few weeks we were given boring jobs such as air-sea reconnaissance from the north of Scotland, involving flying for hours on end over the North Sea, or transporting meteorologists to observe the weather conditions.

On one occasion when coming in to land we hit a seagull, which exploded through the windscreen. The cockpit looked like an abattoir, with blood and feathers scattered in all directions, and Frank, sitting next to me, was hit in the chest by its beak, which penetrated his clothing.

Our landing speed was just 85 miles per hour, so one can envisage the potential damage to a modern jet, landing at 200 miles per hour...

Mess Parties

Some of the diversions of squadron life were our mess parties, held on days when we were stood down from operations, when everyone let their hair down and took part in stupid drunken activities which would never have been countenanced in normal circumstances.

We had a beautiful mess, carpeted and furnished in lavish peacetime style, but on party nights nothing was sacrosanct. For example, two or three tables would be stacked up so that some drunken idiot could decorate the ceiling with shoes dipped in ink, and it would appear as if someone had walked across it...

Needless to say the footprint man quite often fell off, suffering injury, although the drunker he was, the less damage would be sustained.

Daytime visitors were often surprised to find the carpet developing a moving hump, which was our bull-terrier mascot crawling beneath it, trying to retrieve a large brass ashtray which had been pushed there upside down for the purpose.

Up for Promotion

Our station commander, the Earl of Bandon, often joined in our parties, later leaving at the wheel of his car and invariably finishing up in the duck-pond at the end of the road. One day I was ordered to report to his office and when I walked in he was studying some papers.

Glancing up he said, "I understand you would like a commission?"

"Yes please, sir," I replied.

"Good show," he said, and carried on reading.

After a few minutes he looked up, appearing to be surprised that I was still there, and asked: "Is there something else?"

When I replied "No sir" he said "Then cut along Shack."

And that was my successful interview to become an RAF officer!

The 'Thousand Bomber' Raids

As I mentioned previously, by the spring of 1942 No.114 was the very last RAF squadron still equipped with Blenheims. Daylight raids were no longer viable as the latest fighter escorts were unable to lower their speed to the Blenheim's paltry 200 miles per hour, therefore apart from the odd night intruder operations we had no role to play. That was, until Bomber Command, under the newly appointed Air Chief Marshal 'Bomber' Harris, decided that we had enough planes to make up the magic number of 1,000.

Thus on 30th May 1942 the first-ever 'thousand bomber raid' was targeted on Cologne, 114 Squadron being given Bonn night fighter aerodrome to close down while the main force attacked the city for two hours.

After bombing the airfield we headed for home, passing over Cologne, which was a mass of flames.

Our total losses of just over four percent were surprisingly low, so two nights later another 'thousand bomber raid' was launched, this time on Essen.

114 Squadron's target was Andorf aerodrome, which we bombed from 3,000 feet. The flak was sporadic and the only

excitement for Frank, Bill and I was when our port engine failed 250 miles from base.

That was the last time the RAF attempted to use a thousand bombers on one target, because in order to make up the numbers the operation had included numerous training planes and the consequent disruption to the training schedules of pupil pilots had been enormous.

However, as a propaganda exercise for the purposes of boosting British morale at a time when it was greatly needed, it had proved to be a great success; it was also to be our final operation on Blenheims.

Engine Trouble

In June the ground crew tried to find an answer to our frequently recurring engine trouble with first the port and then the starboard engine, until the eventual replacement of both finally solved the problem. Fortunately, these troubles occurred at the end of our tour or Frank, Bill and I may have been accused of 'LMF' (lack of moral fibre) – an RAF term for cowardice.

No 'Gongs' For Me

I was then posted to an Operational Training Unit with a recommendation for a Distinguished Flying Medal (DFM) but this was turned down as on my last 20 operations, unknown to anyone, including myself, I was already a commissioned officer, the irony being that if captured I would have been treated as a non-commissioned officer!

Our Group Captain then changed the recommendation to Distinguished Flying Cross (DFC), which was also turned down on the grounds that as a newly-commissioned officer I did not have sufficient experience of leadership, and such non-immediate awards were given for leadership combined with good work.

However, on an operational squadron, experience, not rank, decided who would do the leading, and I had, in fact, led formations which included much higher ranking personnel than myself, including a Wing Commander and a Squadron Leader, on more than one occasion.

My lack of 'gongs' notwithstanding, after the war, when the Air Ministry revealed that in 1941-2 the average life expectancy of a Blenheim crew was only 5½ hours, I consider myself extremely fortunate to have survived at all, having been on a Blenheim Squadron for over 11 months – twice as long as the usual 'tour' time.

Bicester OTU

At the OTU in Bicester I was an adviser on operational training flights, which meant flying obsolete Avro Ansons on cross-country flights for several hours with five or six trainee navigators on board.

During this period I was also in charge of supervising night-time circuits and landings, which involved standing on the flarepath to guide in the trainee pilots.

After two nights on duty, when four planes crash landed, my nerves were so shot to pieces that I asked the chief instructor to send me back on operations!

As a result I was sent on a flying instructor's course and having passed I joined 'A' Flight, teaching individual pupils in the air how to convert from Oxfords (their training planes) to Blenheims (which were larger, faster aircraft). It was a job which I enjoyed, although it was not without its hair-raising moments...

On one occasion, whilst making a landing approach, my pupil held up the undercarriage lever, which had sheared off as he pushed it down. Having warned control that we were about to land with our wheels up, we were escorted across the airfield by two crash wagons and an ambulance, neither of which were needed, thank God!

At a later date, when practising low-flying, I went through some high tension cables, bringing back six feet of cable embedded in my tail-fin. For this I was court-martialled, pleaded guilty and was sentenced to a reprimand of the loss of nine months seniority, although the episode was seemingly soon forgotten and my promotion to Flight Lieutenant came through 18 months after I was commissioned, which was the normal length of time.

My Funeral Fiasco

In those days one had to be prepared for anything, so when a pupil suffered a fatal crash I found myself ordered to take charge of the funeral.

Normally the duty of the most senior officer, who in this case was our Wing Commander, it had been passed down via our Squadron leader and so on until it reached Pilot Officer Shackleton, who had no one to pass it on to and was therefore lumbered with the job.

On the day of the funeral, the cortege formed up with me at its head, followed by the hearse and a car containing the unfortunate student pilot's relatives.

But as we approached the chapel, which also functioned as a gymnasium, it was found to be locked, whereupon an airman was sent off post-haste on a bicycle to fetch the key from the guardroom.

The next 15 to 20 minutes seemed like a lifetime to me as we played for time by taking the flowers off the hearse and rearranging them before putting them back again.

Finally, when I could think of nothing else to suggest, we removed the coffin and put it very, very slowly on the pall-bearers' shoulders.

Moving at a snail's pace we approached the chapel doors, arriving simultaneously with the breathless airman – plus the key.

Needless to say, even after all these years, whenever I attend a funeral the memory of that incident still remains...

Catering Capers

Before my commission came through, while still a sergeant, I mentioned to the station catering officer that we all thought the food was inadequate. He told me that as operational air crews we were entitled to more rations – of sugar and butter, for example – than anyone else and that being only a few in number and away from the main station, we always received plenty. He asked me if I would be prepared to check what we were entitled to against what we actually received and I soon discovered that a significant proportion of our rations were being systematically 'liberated' by the civilian cooks, who lived locally. Threatening to bring in the police saw an immediate improvement, however.

When my commission came through my commanding officer told me that as I had done such a good job for the sergeants I could now take on the officers' mess – a duty which followed me for the rest of my time in the service and included mess parties. Thus, as a part-time catering officer in charge of meals, I used to discuss our menus with the cooks and on being told that dried scrambled eggs were served almost daily for breakfast I suggested that as we were a small mess of about 20 we might have omelettes. The next morning before sitting down to my own breakfast I saw on the plates of fellow officers some yellow cubes with the consistency of rubber being despondently pushed around by forks. Confronting the large WAAF cook I hesitantly enquired what had become of the omelettes.

"You have *got* omelettes!" she snapped, and opening an oven door revealed a large baking tin full of a yellow, rubbery substance which had been cut into neat squares. We reverted to scrambled eggs after that.

In the middle of 1942 the Germans began a new campaign of launching V1 and V2 rockets at the South of England, including, of course, London, from where thousands were evacuated, and this resulted in large stocks of rationed produce being unclaimed. A party was planned involving all the local bigwigs and in my catering officer's role I was told to "make it special". A friend of mine near my Epsom home had several grocery shops and was only too happy to unload some unsold rations of butter and sugar to someone he could trust, but my father, upon driving me to the station to catch my train back to Cranfield, was not pleased when he discovered what we were carrying, complaining: "I could have finished up in jail if we had been stopped!"

I knew that plenty of eggs would be available from farmer friends in Norfolk, the only snag being to get them to Bedfordshire. Then I had the brainwave of writing to Alec, a friend of mine who was the Registrar of Fakenham, to ask him to collect the farmer's eggs and deliver them to the RAF at West Raynham, where I would pick them up in a Blenheim. (This, I might add, was accomplished without a single egg being broken!)

The Cranfield party was a huge success, particularly some vol-au-vents made with puff pastry which melted in one's mouth. Alec remained a friend, although our relationship was a bit strained for a while afterwards. This was due to the fact that in addition to being a Registrar Alec was also the local Food Officer, so my hastily scribbled request for 12 dozen eggs to be delivered to the nearby airstrip had made his hair stand on end! It had been opened by his secretary, so he made a great show of throwing it straight into the wastepaper basket, exclaiming, "You know what those RAF chaps are like – it must be their idea of a joke!"

Conversion to Mosquitos

At the end of two years instructing I applied for a transfer back to an operational squadron and as a result I was posted to an OTU near Shrewsbury to convert onto Mosquitos.

A revolutionary aeroplane at that time, the De Havilland Mosquito had an all-wooden fuselage, two Rolls-Royce engines, eight machine guns and four cannons, all forward firing. The cruising speed was 280 miles per hour with a maximum of 360 miles per hour – about the same as the German Messerschmitt 109 or the RAF's Spitfires.

When the guns and cannons were removed it could carry 4,000lbs of bombs, and as the war progressed the Mosquito proved to be equally versatile and efficient as the four-engined Lancaster. A truly amazing all-purpose plane, the Mossie's most successful role was that of a high-speed, long-range bomber but it could also be used as a night-fighter flying faster than many of its British and German counterparts. Not surprisingly it was hailed by the press as "the wooden wonder".

At the beginning of my course converting from Blenheims to Mosquitos I climbed into a dual-control aircraft with an instructor. We were airborne and I had just taken over when suddenly the starboard engine failed. Calmly, my instructor told me to carry on flying and at 2,000 feet to turn into the dead engine. This was totally against everything I had been taught, as in the old Blenheim, if one turned into a dead engine the plane would probably have gone into a fatal spin. Later, when I tentatively queried this with the instructor, he laughed and said, "Mosquitoes fly nearly as well on one engine as on two ... if you just remember that they have a high stalling speed and therefore to keep an even closer eye than usual on the air-speed indicator."

To my eternal disappointment, on the day I was posted to a Mosquito Squadron I was urgently admitted to hospital with what was thought to the food poisoning but which later proved to be a gastric ulcer. This, ultimately, resulted in my being invalided out of the Royal Air Force.

Another Somewhat Hairy Air Test

Some of one's worst surprises did not always occur when actually flying. I discovered as much on one occasion when I collected a plane from dispersal to air test it.

Following a circuit and landing I taxied around the perimeter for another take-off when I noticed several groundcrew jumping up and down and waving furiously.

Not surprising really. On grinding to a halt I discovered a mechanic clinging like a limpet to the rear of the fuselage!

Apparently, he had not expected me to take off and had hitched a lift, hoping simply to cross the airfield!

At one stage we wondered whether we would ever be able to separate him from the aeroplane, as prising his petrified fingers open proved to be quite a difficult task after such a traumatic experience.

As a matter of fact, I didn't feel too good either...

Condolence and Embarrassment

The losses on a Blenheim squadron at that time were pretty horrendous, so one never expected friendships to last. One exception for me was Tommy Thompson. We had joined our first OTU together and both finished up on 114 Squadron. We were both on the daylight raid over Norway (mentioned earlier) but tragically he was one of the unlucky victims of the collision over Herdla.

Tommy's wife wrote to me some time later to say she would like us to meet, as all she had received from the Air Ministry was an official message to say that her husband was 'missing'.

We met at the Randolph Hotel in Oxford, where over dinner we sadly discussed Tommy's courage, cheerfulness and subsequent demise.

The meal finished and we decided that the theatre or pictures might be a comfort and upon making enquiries at reception I was told by the desk clerk that he happened to have two tickets for the theatre that night, given to him by a prematurely departing guest. The show was *Start a New Note* – then showing to full houses prior to its premiere at the Prince of Wales Theatre in London.

After arriving in the foyer we were taken to our seats, which were conspicuously in the centre of the front row of the stalls, but just before the overture began I was approached by the usher, who asked to inspect our tickets.

I was horrified and embarrassed when he then asked me to accompany him to see the manager, who was with a policeman.

After answering numerous questions I was informed that my tickets had been stolen by the cloakroom attendant at the Randolph Hotel, who had apparently been stealing from coats and bags left there and had passed the tickets on to his friend the desk clerk, in exchange for a 'cut' of the proceeds.

The cloakroom attendant would probably never have been discovered had he not been greedy regarding those theatre tickets; it emerged that he was an Austrian refugee and his fate was subsequently to be deported.

Happily for Mrs Thompson and myself, the theatre manager gave us replacement tickets and we thoroughly enjoyed the show after all...

Farewell to 'L' for London

I have never been a superstitious person but I must confess that when flying my old 'L' for London Blenheim I always felt an inexplicable sense of security, so I was saddened when in March 1942, upon returning from home leave, I was told that it had not come back from night operations over Schipol.

My dejection embraced the ill-fated pilot and crew, of course, for whom 'L' had not been the lucky aeroplane it had been for me.

Another Ambition Realised

In 1945 my five years as a wartime pilot finally came to an end and ever since then I have considered myself incredibly fortunate to have survived through a period when one never really expected to live to see one's next leave (and that was at a time when operational flying crews were given seven days every six weeks instead of the normal 12 weeks), let alone witness the end of hostilities.

Upon my discharge I threw myself into charity work for the subsequent 50-odd years, my way of saying 'thank you' for being spared when so many young men had been killed.

Now the memories of those action-packed war years often come flooding back into my mind, one memorable occasion being when I fulfilled the childhood ambition (shared by many other little boys) to drive a steam-powered railway engine.

My opportunity came when on leave and standing on the platform of Aylesbury station. For some reason a locomotive had been disconnected from the main body of the train and on the spur of the moment I told the driver that if he would let me "have a go" at driving it I would reciprocate by taking him up in an aeroplane sometime.

Thus, an immaculately uniformed RAF officer climbed up onto the footplate and half an hour later a dirty, scruffy but very happy one descended. Wearing an extremely self-satisfied expression he hastily headed to the nearest toilet for a major clean-up!

A Glow in the Dark

Little things can often trigger one's memory, such as when I see cigarettes glowing in the dark...

Many of our operations were flown in formation and it was the unwritten rule that smoking never took place until we were well away from the enemy coast and homeward bound.

At that point one would suddenly spot the flare of a match in the leader's cockpit, which would immediately be followed by comforting flashes of light throughout the whole formation.

Lecherous Low Flying

Whenever tempted to shake my head at the escapades of 'modern youth' I try to remember that the normal, healthy young men of 2 Group were no less interested in the opposite sex.

For example, when joining the squadron we had to practise a lot of low-flying, so low that we had to weave around trees instead of passing over them.

On one leg across country we passed over a group of land girls who, taking advantage of a very hot summer, were working topless out in the fields.

This important piece of 'intelligence' was quickly passed around and their exact position was carefully charted.

And of course it remained a focal point for many low-level flights thereafter...

Comrades in Arms

No doubt as a result of our dangerous circumstances there was a strong comradeship throughout the squadron – a sense of togetherness I have rarely experienced with a group of men during the peaceful postwar years since.

In the Forties radar-less Blenheims required fairly good weather conditions for flying – one reason alone being so that we could navigate in the UK by following railway lines.

Thus, inclement weather would find us huddled up in the crew room, awaiting the order to scramble, playing cards.

Poker was popular, but so many chaps lost their pay that Bridge became the number one favourite and my love of that game has lasted ever since.

Not Such a Brilliant Idea

Mentioning radar-less Blenheims and basic navigation reminds me of an unforgettable occasion experienced by friends on my squadron.

It happened on the day when Johnny Glen, a pilot, was due to go on night operations, so, as was the custom, he and one of his crew boarded their Blenheim to carry out a night flying test (NFT) to make sure that all was in good working order prior to that evening's operation. Their navigator was not with them because they planned to make just a couple of circuits over the airfield with Johnny checking the engines while Bob, his gun and wireless operator, checked that the guns, compass and radio (the latter being the Blenheim's navigation equipment) were all functioning properly.

It was a beautiful sunny afternoon in winter, so when a sea mist rolled in from the north it took them completely by surprise. Suddenly blinded by thick fog, Johnny flew around helplessly for a couple of hours, hoping it would clear.

Unfortunately, visibility worsened and with dusk approaching Johnny had what he later described as "a brilliant idea".

He told Bob to bale out and "as soon as you touch terra firma, old boy, note the time then contact Fighter Command, telling them that I shall be flying due north at 180 miles per hour and ask them to send up a plane to lead me down." (Fighters were all equipped with radar, so they were confident of a quick rescue...)

Sadly for both men they had not realised that they were flying over The Wash and consequently when Bob baled out he was not only given a ducking but also it was some hours before he was lucky enough to be rescued by a fishing boat.

Meanwhile Johnny was steadily flying due north at 180 miles per hour and beginning to panic, for as darkness fell so did his petrol gauge.

Descending to a very low level he spotted a beach, which appeared to be free from the usual wartime obstacles, and decided to land there...

Feeling thankful that he and his plane were still in one piece he emerged from his cockpit to hear frantic warning shouts from the coastguard. Poor old Johnny had landed in the middle of a mined beach and had to be escorted to safety by the Army, all in the state of red alert.

Thus ended a memorable night flying test and one which proved that even the most brilliant ideas do not always go according to plan!

Brazening it Out in the Blitz

One of my most vivid memories of the war is of walking across London Bridge during an air raid, whilst I was on home leave.

All buses and trains had stopped and there was not a soul in sight as anti-aircraft guns were thumping away and bombs were dropping all around.

I was really scared but did not think it would look right for an RAF officer pilot to be seen running for shelter.

So, with apparent calm and unhurried determination, I walked steadfastly on...

True Fighting Spirit

During those war years, of course, one saw some truly amazing examples of what I consider to be 'raw courage', such as when, during our final days at OTU, the planes were loaded with high explosive bombs instead of the usual practice ones, to drop on a UK range.

There were several Polish pilots on our training course and upon taking off one of them disappeared in the direction of Germany, never to be seen again.

One of his compatriots later explained:

"He told me he was not going to waste live bombs when they could serve a really useful purpose."

'Friendly' Fire

During recent wars much publicity has been given to casualties resulting from so-called 'friendly' fire, yet it is often forgotten that being shot down by one's own side was not unknown during the Second World War.

For RAF aircrews the culprit was often our own somewhat over-zealous Royal Navy. When asked why this occurred when we always displayed the correct 'colours of the day' the Royal Navy replied that they never took too much notice of the latter, knowing that the enemy would often guess our colours and display them also, and it must be admitted that when we flew over German ships we would always run through all the colours, hoping to display the ones they had chosen for the day.

It should also be mentioned that our casualties when flying over the enemy were often fewer than over our own navy, because if we flew over without deviating the Germans would often keep a low profile, hoping we had not spotted them, whereas our own ships tended to shoot at anything they were not absolutely sure of. Not surprisingly remarks such as "the Royal Navy's motto is 'fire first, ask questions later'" were circulating in our mess and at one stage the 'friendly' fire became so serious that an Air Marshal from the Air Ministry spoke to both the Navy and the RAF on the subject. The former were ordered not to be so trigger-happy unless they were really sure as to who was flying overhead, while the RAF were warned not always to take evasive action over our own ships, as this could be interpreted as a hostile act and arouse suspicion.

Needless to say, we believed that if we did not take evasive action we would be shot down anyway, and during that time I remember at least two of our crews being lost as a result.

The Art of Escaping

As a part of our training we were taught how to escape capture in enemy territory. For this exercise we were taken in buses with the side windows blacked-out for 10 or 15 miles and told to find our way back to base.

We were each given a hand-held compass and a local quarter-inch map, which would have been fine if one had any idea of one's starting point. However, as a wartime precaution all signposts had been removed in order to 'confuse the enemy' (I don't know about the enemy but I for one was completely confused!).

The local police and Home Guard were all out enthusiastically looking for us (to have the kudos of "capturing" an RAF pilot) so those lessons were always a hair-raising experience.

On one such occasion I was feeling rather pleased with myself, having moved stealthily many miles across country in the direction of our base without being spotted.

"The secret is to crawl along the bottom of the hedgerows," I told myself smugly, when suddenly I was ambushed and taken prisoner.

"How on earth did you know where I was?" I demanded to know, while sipping a most welcome cup of tea.

"Easy," came the reply, "we just sat back and watched the birds fly up every time you moved!"

Food and Fuel Shortages

Never having liked the taste of alcohol I would often skip evenings in the mess bar and pop out for dinner at The Crown pub in Fakenham or to a small restaurant nearby, where I could enjoy bacon, eggs, sausages and chips, which were quite a rarity in those days. It was on one of those solitary outings I met a charming local couple, Alec and Trixie.

Alec was a Registrar of weddings, etc and was also a wartime Food Officer (as mentioned in a previous story). I was delighted when they invited me to their house for a meal, for they were both interesting and amusing hosts and for the first time in almost a year I was able to savour the comforts of a proper home, which worked wonders for my morale.

Of course I was always aware of Alec's official position and tried never to embarrass him, although I did not always succeed (see the story recounted earlier). For example, although petrol was limited and rationing strict, due to my father owning a large fruit and vegetable business, which had a big fleet of petrol-driven lorries, I always had enough petrol coupons for travelling to Fakenham or Norwich whenever I felt like it, and when one evening Alec remarked that petrol rationing never seem to affect me, I said that as part of my RAF duties I 'had to visit our satellite stations by car from time to time'...

One night, in an effort to repay some of their kindness, I invited Alec and Trixie to dinner at my favourite little restaurant. I ordered steak and chips and my guests did the same, but a few minutes later our waitress whispered in my ear that the manager would like to see me "round the back".

Looking extremely flustered, the manager asked, "Do you know that your guest is the Food Officer?" to which I replied, "Of course!"

The manager's voice then dropped to a whisper as he informed me, "We should not be serving steak. It has not been allocated to us officially for some time."

"Everything will be quite all right," I assured him, "just leave it with me..."

Upon returning to my table I asked Alec if he was 'on duty' to which he responded with a very cheerful "No".

"Good," I said, "because behind-the-scenes they are in a flap due to serving illicit steak when they know who you are."

"No worries!" laughed Alec, "I have bigger problems to be concerned about at present," at which point the steaks arrived and we enjoyed them immensely.

After the war, when I made business trips to Norfolk growers I would call on Alec and Trixie with gifts of citrus fruits, which were still in short supply, and therefore rationed.

To salve Alec's conscience I explained that due to so many people having been evacuated from London during the bombing there was a surplus of perishable foods to be got rid of.

In fact, due to my parents wholesale fruit and vegetable business my family had never suffered diet-wise during the war years and the lean times which followed. For them, money only played a minor role when acquiring goods in short supply, as the age-old barter system took over, with sugar, butter and meat appearing in my mother's shopping basket, which had left home filled with fruit and vegetables.

Our 'Local'

My Squadron adopted The Crown at Fakenham as its 'local', to which we made visits about once or twice a month. We would all squeeze into the station minibus and, being the only non-drinker, I would be assigned to the driving, of course.

In those days I would order ginger ale, bitter lemon having not been invented, so whenever "Time gentlemen please" found us sitting around a table deep in conversation, everyone's glass would disappear out of sight except mine. Then, when the local police, desperate to make a catch, raided the joint (as they say nowadays) they would home in on my solitary ginger ale and would be somewhat irritated to discover that it contained not a trace of alcohol.

In spite of having driven since I was 16, returning to base during the blackout was always a challenge, with frequent sea mists whirling around, plus an occasional cow or tractor blocking the road. Our commanding officer always joined us and as a precaution (just in case we were involved in an accident) he made it a rule that only a small group at a time could leave base for an evening out.

Weasenham Hall

As I mentioned previously, Weasenham Hall, where we were billeted at West Raynham, was a beautiful 18th century mansion, surrounded by its own farmland. Being Norfolk, the game shooting was excellent, so pheasants and partridges appeared regularly in our mess, which made a delicious change from the usual RAF wartime fare.

The owners of the estate, a charming couple who looked upon their move into the servants quarters as "the least we can do" were responsible for the above, saying that helping to keep 114 Squadron well fed and comfortably housed was their contribution to the war effort.

Norfolk-Style Security

"Careless talk costs lives" was firmly ingrained on all our consciences and we would never impart information to any of our local civilian friends, but we soon discovered that away from London such security measures seemed to be unknown.

We would frequently overhear villagers discussing our latest (top-secret) bombing raids, including our targets and the number of casualties, if there had been any...

On Leave

Prior to joining the RAF, when still at home, living with my parents, I decided that a good way to meet members of the opposite sex would be to join the local ballroom dancing class.

One of our teachers was Dorothy Dodds, about 20 years older than her young pupils, but full of life and in possession of a (very necessary) sense of humour.

Being extremely good at her job she passed on her enormous enthusiasm and soon had us tripping the light fantastic to the toe-tapping music of Victor Sylvester and other contemporary favourites.

Later, as a raw recruit in the service, I was posted to Torquay, where I was feeling very lonely and homesick, so imagine my delight when I bumped into Dorothy again on the seafront one morning, her London-based business having been evacuated to the seaside.

What a morale-booster she was, being able to lift my spirits and make me laugh at a time when I needed just such a friend, and to this day I remember her with great affection and gratitude.

I had been in the RAF for 11 months before I got my first leave of just seven days. Upon arriving home I was disappointed to discover that my chums were away in the forces and most unattached girls were spoken for, therefore one night when I decided to go to the local dance I thought Christmas had arrived early when I discovered that girls outnumbered boys by six to one!

The trouble was, however, that practically every dance was a ladies 'excuse me' waltz. When I nervously tried to remember Dorothy's dancing lessons, what should have been 1-2-3 became 3-2-1 and by the time I had sorted myself out my partner had invariably been 'excused', leaving me to start all over again...

After about an hour the air raid sirens sounded and we were all herded into shelters. Some time later the 'all clear' went and as we climbed the stairs to leave the shelter I began chatting to an extremely buxom young lady who had been one of my dancing partners earlier.

Suddenly, however, she fainted, with me just managing to catch her before she hit the floor.

Upon carrying her back up to the street I found the blackout door firmly closed, so after carefully lowering her to the ground I knocked on it with whatever strength I could still muster, whilst getting my breath back.

My passage cleared at last, I scooped up my corpulent friend once more, who now felt as if she weighed more than a ton, and staggered out into the night, hoping to hail a taxi.

One finally arrived just as she was coming round, and when I discovered that she only lived a couple of miles from my parents' house I went with her as her escort (handing her over to an extremely suspicious-looking mother) then, having no more money, I paid the taxi fare and returned home on foot.

A memorable leave, to say the least, and one which left me trying to eke out my pay for the rest of the month!

For some time afterwards I had to endure comments from my friends regarding how lucky I was having had the company of a young lady for a whole evening and then having taken her home afterwards – if only they knew!

Speeding into Trouble

Whenever I had an odd day off at West Raynham I would try to go home to London, which involved a round trip of approximately 150 miles.

Needless to say I was always in a hurry and although there was very little traffic about there were plenty of roadside speed traps.

Over a twelve-month period I was stopped for speeding 29 times, although I usually managed to talk my way out of trouble.

If on my way homeward, I would murmur some excuse about "a family crisis" whereas if driving back to base I would explain that I had been suddenly 'recalled to the Squadron'.

On the one occasion that I was issued with a summons I pleaded guilty, but in court the magistrate dismissed the charge, telling the police that he thought they must have "more important things to do than harass RAF pilots".

Instructing

The instructor's course, mentioned earlier in my account, was very hard work, especially the flying parts, which previously I had found easy.

As a budding instructor I suddenly realised that I was being scrutinised every step of the way, from the moment of climbing into the cockpit, strapping myself in and plugging in the microphone (which was connected to a radio telephone at base).

Out of the 12 of us who began the course only five survived to the end, an interesting mix of airmen from a Wing Commander down the ranks to me, plus one other sergeant, yet whilst under instruction we were all treated as equals, which was very pleasing.

Once on board the aircraft, in our case a Blenheim, there was never any time to relax, as, for example, it would have been arranged that in the middle of takeoff one engine would suddenly fail, or on the final approach to landing warning lights would flash on and off and the klaxon would sound, indicating that our wheels were still up.

We were taught how to handle the above situations, of course, and more importantly how to pass on this knowledge to our pupils.

On the subject of landing we were told of how one pupil, going solo, had completely ignored both warning lights and klaxon, bringing his plane in to land and wiping off its undercarriage while doing so.

"Why on earth did you ignore the controller's orders to go round again as your wheels were still retracted?" the chief instructor demanded of the quaking young airmen, who thankfully was in better shape than his aircraft.

"Well sir," he replied, "the klaxon was making more noise than a loud car horn so I could not hear anything on my radio telephone."

Whilst on the instructor's course I enjoyed the opportunity of flying Bostons, which were beginning to replace the now outdated Blenheim, being much faster and able to carry a heavier bombload. As well as the above advantages, Bostons were more streamlined than Bleheims, Wellingtons and Whitleys and needed a crew of only two, a pilot plus a navigator/bomb-aimer, compared with three to five in other bombers mentioned.

In 1941-42 the Boston was replaced by the DeHavilland Mosquito, which also had a crew of only two and, like the

Boston, was fast compared with other aircraft at that time so a rear gunner was considered a luxury superfluous to requirements.

As previously mentioned my pupils would all have their wings and be at the stage in their flying career when they were ready to specialise, so my task was to instruct them in how to become proficient pilots on a Blenheim squadron.

Having been rated "above average" at the end of my instructor's course I left happy and proud to have had the opportunity of teaching – a job which I came to enjoy enormously.

Needless to say, psychology played a vital role in my approach to each individual pupil, as their personalities differed greatly.

Some young men would jump jauntily into the cockpit beside me and I would know by their attitude that in their eyes they were budding Douglas Bader's. With that type I tended to be firm from the outset and was highly critical of any mistakes they made, at times aiming to puncture their ego. This might sound harsh, but I knew that my discouraging their bravado could save their lives in the future.

Conversely, when the opposite type of pupil came under my instruction, their confidence had to be boosted by my praising their (almost) every move. Most of my pupils could not wait to be told to "go solo" but those who were under-confident would usually stall for time, saying, for example, "Let's just do a couple more circuits together".

If I refused, insisting that my pupil should go straight up alone, I would suffer a nagging fear that he really may not be ready and that I had just send him to a premature death.

Fortunately, this never happened, perhaps because in cases where I felt a pupil really was lacking enough confidence to fly a Blenheim solo I would inform our chief flying instructor. The CFI would then take my chap on a flight and assess the situation, with years of teaching experience behind him to aid his decision.

Under- and over-confidence were not the only problems I came across while instructing, of course, and on one occasion I encountered a case of colour-blindness. I should explain that when landing in poor visibility or at night, a glide path indicator was essential to ensure the correct angle of descent, the indicator giving out three beams of light, in green, orange and red. If the pilot's angle of descent was correct he saw green; if too high he saw orange; if too low it was red. Providing the right air speed was maintained, all he had to focus on was clearing the boundary, keeping the plane straight – i.e. not swinging to the left or right – and closing the throttles ready to land.

One day I was practising landings with a new pupil when I discovered that he seemed unable to distinguish between the colours of the glide path indicator lights. Most concerned about this I put him up for a test flight with the CFI, after which he was sent for a medical, including an eye test for colour blindness, which he failed.

Upon my expressing surprise that the condition had not been diagnosed during previous training flights, I was told that while flying low speed aircraft such as the Oxford, the pupil had got away with the condition, but when he changed to the higher speed Blenheim his eyes had less time to differentiate between the colours, even when slowing up to land.

Once on the runway, well controlled taxiing and parking correctly were of the utmost importance and I frequently reminded my charges that when on an operational squadron, whilst returning their planes to base well peppered with enemy shrapnel might earn them a gong, nudging another Blenheim while on the move back home – e.g. scraping a wing – would result in them being ordered to wash down aeroplanes for a week.

Whilst serving as an instructor I tried to remember what it had been like being a pupil myself and which of my various teachers I had preferred, and why, in order that I could endeavour to emulate the best ones. Needless to say, one always had to be ready to take over from one's pupil at a moment's notice to prevent disaster, yet never to move in too soon, as this could undermine their confidence. Maintaining that fine balance was not always easy, sometimes straining one's nerves as much as any bombing operation ever did.

Why I Didn't Go to Malta

Although my first posting was to a Blenheim squadron based at West Raynham in Norfolk, I should, in fact, have been sent to Malta. However, I had suffered with dermatitis from an early age, which seemed to be exacerbated by strong sunlight and consequently I had never at any time sun-bathed and during the summer months was forced to wear a wide-brimmed hat.

Aware that I could have problems in sunny Malta I consulted our M.O., who said that if I really was allergic to the sun's rays the posting would not be a good idea.

Thus Malta was put on hold while I underwent a series of tests, which included a 20-minute trial beneath a sunlamp, following which I had to be admitted to the sick-bay, where I spent a fortnight recovering from extensive skin rashes.

Upon being discharged I was declared 'unfit for the tropics and subtropics' and was subsequently posted to West Raynham and 114 Squadron.

On my last night at OTU prior to leaving for Norfolk I was in the mess when a furious-looking fellow pilot stormed up to me.

"Do you realise that you will almost certainly be responsible for sending me to my death?" he demanded, and noting my blank, uncomprehending expression, continued, "I am being posted to Malta in your place and I do not need to remind you of our casualty figures out there!"

He departed as quickly as he had come, leaving me with a horrible feeling of guilt that what he said could be true, so you can imagine just how relieved I felt when one year later the same chap, now a Pilot Officer, walked jauntily into our mess. Furthermore, in the post-war years, having earned a DFC and a DFM he had a most fascinating book published concerning his wartime exploits on that Mediterranean island.

No Soft Option

As it happened, I was soon to discover that our casualty figures during operations from Norfolk were absolutely horrendous. Upon arriving from OTU, we new airmen, plus the aircrews already at West Raynham, made up a total of 13, so our maximum effort for the first months had always to be the entire squadron. You never had to wonder whether or not you were on the battle order – you were! Fortunately, however, we soon reached the stage when a steady trickle of fresh crews were coming through, which were desperately required to keep our numbers constant and 114 Squadron airborne.

Nowadays I look back in total amazement at our seemingly cold-blooded, callous behaviour; upon noticing a colleague's absence from both the mess and his bunker following an operation we had no qualms in sharing out his cigarettes, chocolate, etc.

Since most of our bombing raids at that time were low-level and in daylight one did not worry about becoming a prisoner of war. So far as we were concerned, there were only two options: to return and survive or not to return and die.

However, at Group Headquarters the powers-that-be were more optimistic and at our final briefing prior to every operation over enemy territory an 'escape kit' was issued to all aircrews in case they were forced down or managed to bale out safely. The kit consisted of a map printed on silk, which looked like a handkerchief, a small compass to be worn as a button, field rations which included chocolate and malted milk tablets and finally benzedrine tablets to help one stay awake. With the kit would also be some foreign currency, depending upon our destination, to be hidden in our flying boots.

Inevitably, it became apparent to headquarters that losses were extremely serious and a change would have to be made. Our first inkling of this came when we began to practise low-level flying on moonlit nights. For those of us on Blenheims either daylight or moonlight was essential because with no sophisticated radar and a limited radio range of only about five miles, visibility had to be good. Fortunately, the change to night flying did cut down our death toll and we felt relieved at HQ's decision.

Bombing St Albans – With Soot!

Whenever I recall practising low-level flying over buildings I cannot help but remember the time when I was a newly-fledged pilot at Upwood OTU and busily bonding with Frank Eyres, my navigator/bomb-aimer and Bill Kennedy my wireless operator/air-gunner. In order to assist new RAF airmen with their low-level bombing skills an exercise had been devised whereby there was an imaginary war between the UK's north and south.

Loaded up with bags of soot to represent bombs, we pupils from training units around the country had to try to close routes between the north and south by bombing roads and prime targets in strategically-placed towns. Neutral adjudicators were on-site to decide whether one had been successful or not, depending upon the type of effective evasive action taken, combined with the level of accuracy of one's 'bombs'.

Frank, Bill and I were given St Albans as our target and being a sunny Saturday morning the market was teeming with happy shoppers. Not for long, however, as soon Bill was enthusiastically dropping bags of soot over the side whenever Frank told him to and, not surprisingly, the RAF became rather unpopular with the civilians of St Albans!

I cannot recall how we 'scored' in this exercise, but remembering it never fails to make me chuckle.

Many years after the war, one of our employees recalled having been in St Albans on that particular day and being suddenly 'bombed' by bags of soot.

I hardly liked to tell him that I had been part of that operation.

Life at Various Bases

Earlier in this account you will have read that I was posted to RAF Lossiemouth in Scotland to join a combined operation to German-occupied Norway. It being December, Lossiemouth was extremely cold, but it's freezing temperatures were modified by the warmth and friendliness of our Scottish counterparts. They gave us a wonderful welcome and were great fun, and soon jokes were flying backwards and forwards between Scots and English aircrews, with teasing and cheery banter, fuelled by the fact that we were all enthusiastic young airmen, thrown together in a time of crisis.

Although Lossiemouth was a main pre-war aerodrome, we slept in Nissen huts, which were erected to house 'extras' such as ourselves. However, while our accommodation was pretty basic the main mess was extremely comfortable and the food in Scotland proved vastly superior to that which we were used to south of the border.

Rich, tasty porridge, hot scones with butter, jam and (yes!) cream, plus mouthwatering Scottish kippers regularly featured in our menus and we even enjoyed some delicious, tender cuts of Highland beef. Needless to say, it was no hardship to be based there over Hogmanay when, with a blizzard blowing, New Year's Eve was a very wild night in all respects.

Whilst writing of different bases, my thoughts go back to Bicester in Oxfordshire. Like Lossiemouth, Bicester had been a pre-war aerodrome, so was similarly comfortable and staffed by 'regulars', who looked down on us "upstarts". However, my colleagues and I accepted our lowly status cheerfully, especially when evenings off meant that we could descend upon the 'Sampson and Hercules', a dancehall in Oxford only about 18 miles from base. At the time there were so many smartly-uniformed male RAF personnel in that part of the world that there were hardly enough girls to go round, but we always enjoyed ourselves nevertheless.

Sadly for us, the comforts of Bicester were short-lived and we were soon shunted off in an RAF bus to Hinton-in-the-Hedges, a satellite of Bicester with concrete runways 200 yards long, which seemed like the end of the earth, where we slept in Nissen huts warmed by a solitary coal-fired heater. In winter one either froze or cooked, depending on one's distance from the sole source of heat and one's level in the two-tiered bunks.

Our meals were served in a satellite mess and although we got the same food as the main mess in Bicester it was somewhat colder, having been cooked in the latter place and sent over.

As mentioned previously, following two years of instructing I was sent to an OTU at High Ercall near Shrewsbury to convert to Mosquitos. Accommodation-wise things followed the same pattern as at other bases. We began at Shrewsbury's commodious main aerodrome, where the mess was bustling with regular peacetime personnel, but later overflowed to the satellite of High Ercall, with Nissen huts again...

Everything is relative, of course, and I must say that one certainly appreciated the comforts of pre-war RAF messes following those huts.

Leaving 114 Squadron

114 Squadron was part of '2 Group', the RAF's light bomber section, and had been 'home' to my crew – Bill, Frank and myself – since our first meeting in May 1941 until June 1942. Then, along with many of our colleagues, we had finished our tour of operations (29 in all) and feeling relieved and somewhat surprised to have come out of it alive we were looking forward to a break from operational flying.

There would be a general upheaval anyway, as 114 Squadron was to be posted to the Middle East, therefore a big mess party, so far as we were concerned, was essential. That party was the best ever, but was followed by something of an anticlimactic period during which we solemnly reflected on what being part of 114 Squadron had meant to us all.

My colleagues and I had, of course, worked and played together in every type of weather. There had been hot summer days when, with the sleeves of one's battledress rolled up one would play cricket on the edge of the airstrip while waiting to go on Ops, when to have hit a six immediately prior to climbing into the cockpit did wonders for one's morale! Being a left-arm bowler of modest repute I never experienced the above, but somewhat smugly, I always enjoyed getting somebody out just before takeoff.

During the winter, when everything was covered in snow, the whole station would be ordered to turn out and remove it, both from the planes and the runways to keep our aerodrome open. On these occasions aircrew and ground-staff worked side-by-side and not surprisingly there was always a bit of rough-and-tumble in the white stuff, with well-aimed snowballs flying around, followed by (good natured) shouts of anguish.

Summer or winter, card games were popular, with Poker being the favourite. However, the gambling instinct was so strong in some members of the Squadron that they would be stony broke as soon as they received their pay (at that time from about twenty-two shillings and sixpence per day, depending on rank) so they then had nothing left for necessary stamps, phone calls, etc. At last our Wing Commander said enough was enough and encouraged us to change to Bridge, which luckily most of us preferred to Poker from the point of view of interest and satisfaction, so we had some good rubbers.

There was a communal wireless in the mess and as most of us enjoyed the same programmes, arguments were unknown. The news was of paramount importance, closely followed by ITMA, which never failed to produce roars of laughter. The station's newspapers were delivered daily, which we always read from the back, starting with the all-important sports section, then moving on to the comic strips such as 'Jane' – scantily clad and everyone's sweet-heart. Only at the end would we concentrate on the serious news of the day – we young men had certain priorities to maintain...

In spite of it being wartime, the Norfolk postal service was extremely dependable, so regular, newsy letters from home became an eagerly-awaited event. When a chap would quietly announce that his parents' house had been bombed, however, we understood his sadness, but never dwelt upon such tragic events, death and destruction having become part of our young lives in those days. They were something we learned to take in our stride with a positive, optimistic approach which was essential to our overall well-being.

There was a NAAFI shop based at West Raynham, manned by cheerful volunteers who seemed to enjoy their useful job, while we in turn were grateful for their services. After cigarettes, chocolate was next in demand and being aircrew I was delighted to receive extra coupons for the latter, which I loved. Not surprisingly therefore, my chubby five-foot ten-inch frame weighed in at 13 stone, while at the time of writing I tip the scales at a mere 11 stone seven pounds, my wife having strictly rationed my chocolate consumption (wisely) during recent years.

The mess bar was open during the evenings only, but certainly made up for its closed times then! Never having liked the taste of beer or other alcoholic drinks, I always stuck to lemonade or ginger ale, soberly watching as some members of the Squadron steadily became so drunk as to be best described as 'paralytic'. Later they would stagger away to bed to sleep it off and nothing (except, perhaps, their livers) seemed to suffer as a result.

If we had Ops scheduled for the following morning it was an unwritten rule that alcohol was taboo. This worked well unless an unforeseen job came through, such as the morning when we were supposed to be on stand-down but were suddenly ordered to become airborne and pick up a fighter escort about an hour's flight away. As a result of imbibing the previous evening, our usually impeccable formation gradually became scattered all over the sky and I cannot help but wonder what one of today's breathalyser tests would have revealed!

Yes, I reflected, I would miss life on my Squadron and remember it with nostalgia in future years. Of course, it had involved discomfort, fear and at times great sadness. Yes, there had been the inevitable missing of one's kith and kin and of home cooking, while one never had any privacy whatsoever, except when in 'the bog'.

Nothing, however, will ever replace the camaraderie we chaps felt for each other or the special bond between men risking their lives for a common cause. I felt proud and grateful to have been part of 2 Group's 114 Squadron and truly sorry to be saying goodbye.

Flying with our Allies

During the war I not only flew with airmen from all parts of the United Kingdom but also with representatives from allied countries such as Canada, Australia, New Zealand, France, Holland, Poland and the Czech Republic.

I am happy to say that we all gelled together with no particular nationality standing out, although I do remember the Poles as being particularly dedicated in their quest to get at the enemy – alone if necessary. I have mentioned such an example in an earlier story and since that episode precautionary measures were taken – i.e. when practising with live bombs all aircraft piloted by Poles were given only enough petrol to fly over the UK and not enough to reach Germany!

There was only one occasion when I recall language posing a problem and that was once when I was instructing. On that day I had a French pupil and we were practising landings. He was perfectly capable of flying the plane but every time we came in to land his airspeed would be all over the place.

I kept repeating "85" (85 miles per hour being the ideal approach landing speed) as I pointed at the airspeed indicator, but received no response from my pupil. Eventually, I delved back into the recesses of my memory and managed to extract some schoolboy French "Quatre-Vingt Cinque!" I exclaimed suddenly, and it worked like magic, my French pupil reducing his speed and making a textbook landing that day.

Oxygen Deprivation

There is one lesson I learned during my own pilot training course which I will never forget and that was concerning the results of oxygen deficiency...

When we climbed into the cockpit of our aircraft the normal drill was to put on our oxygen masks, which were attached to our microphones, and at 6,000 feet to flip a switch behind us and turn on the oxygen. Throughout my years as a pilot this became second nature to me, thanks to a memorable demonstration back at our first OTU.

Our instructor had explained: "when over 20,000 feet you will have to use oxygen. You will not know that you need it, so we are going to show you how dangerous the effects of oxygen deprivation can be by reducing your supply of oxygen in a controlled, safe, environment."

Thus, one by one, we were told to sit in a decompression chamber holding a writing pad and pencil, our instructions being to write our name and service number on the pad until told to stop. This we did, until being released from the chamber, whereupon we were told at which point our oxygen supply had been reduced. Having felt absolutely nothing at all and being unaware of any change in the atmosphere, we were amazed to see that from that time onwards our writing had progressively turned into complete gibberish.

Mascots & Superstitions

Just as eating large helpings of carrots to help one see in the dark became part of our routine prior to night flying, so did the grabbing of mascots before all takeoffs.

Most members of 114 Squadron carried a lucky mascot such as a rabbit's foot or a special scarf. I never carried a mascot, as such, but always stored my cigarettes in a 'Regency' cigarette tin, which I kept in my breast pocket in the belief that it would be in the right place to deflect any shrapnel and thus save my life.

The Regency tin never did get the chance to fulfil the role of a shield, but during a circus at 10,000 feet over Ostend docks (see my earlier account) a piece of shrapnel pierced my armour plated seat back and lodged itself in the webbing of my parachute harness, worn over my flying suit.

Before leaving base I had pompously assured some newly-arrived crews that we had never suffered losses or indeed seen much enemy action on circuses, which I described to them as "a piece of cake". I am not superstitious, but that was the very last time I ever use that expression prior to take off.

Like many squadrons we had a communal mascot and ours was in the form of a bull terrier called (most appropriately) Simple Simon. He had been adopted by 114 Squadron when a puppy and lived in the mess crew room, offering fun, friendship and, when required, comfort to all.

For visitors to our mess, Simon was a star performer and was also a remarkable retriever. Not only would our dog return his rubber balls and various toys, which we would throw for him, but would also pounce upon matchsticks, cigarette ends and any other rubbish, which he would proudly bring back to the chap who had discarded them.

Needless to say, such antics produced both frustration and amusement – far more of the latter, though – so when one day our happy, popular little friend was almost killed we were horrified.

It happened as follows: in those days the planes had a strip of yellow painted along the ends of the propeller blades so that when the engines were just ticking over people would not walk into them. Poor Simon, upon seeing an idling plane for the first time, noticed the propeller strip, ran over, and jumped up to catch it… whereupon he was hit under the chin, did a backward somersault and flew through the air, landing with his legs pointing skywards. To everybody's relief Simon suffered no lasting damage – but he remained very wary of aeroplanes after that…

Learning to Shoot

When joining the RAF I was completely kitted out with clothing from head to toe by courtesy of His Majesty's Government. Included in the kit were flying boots with tops which could easily be cut off so if one was shot down over enemy territory (and survived) they would look like civilian shoes. The above boots, I may say, were fur-lined, which was much appreciated as there was no heating in a Blenheim cockpit. During the later stages of my wartime service I flew an American Mitchell and was greatly impressed by its 'luxuries', such as a cigarette lighter and ashtray (smoking on all RAF planes was forbidden, although that rule was often ignored), padded arm and headrest and (of course) heating in the cockpit!

Upon becoming an officer I was presented with £50 plus clothing coupons and told to buy my own uniform. Thus, with a very proud father in tow, I visited Austin Reed on Regent Street to purchase my requirements. These included two smart jackets and trousers, a peaked cap as well as a forage cap, shoes, socks, gloves and underwear. It should be mentioned at this point that for me as well as for all my fellow officers before me it was exciting to walk into a gentlemen's outfitters as an ordinary NCO and to walk out as an officer. Therefore, following the usual custom, I bought one set of jacket and trousers "off-the-peg" to wear immediately, but ordered a second set to be tailor-made for formal occasions.

Although £50 does not seem much with which to purchase the above, the cost of living during the 1940s was much less than it is nowadays in proportion to our low wages. For example, a list of my monthly expenditures might have included the following: a seat at the pictures cost sixpence; fish and chips, with the fish at sixpence and chips at one penny; cigarettes at sixpence for 10; ginger ale at fourpence per glass; petrol at approximately ninepence per gallon and a newspaper just one penny.

Even at the above prices, however, making my pay last (two shillings and sixpence a day, when a new recruit) for a whole month required careful calculations. As an officer (Flight Lieutenant) I received 22 shillings and sixpence per day, so things became easier and I enjoyed wearing my smart new uniform, of course, although after the novelty wore off continually returning salutes became rather a bore and one learned to pretend not to notice lower ranks saluting.

Only officers were issued with revolvers and when I was commissioned I was given a service revolver plus a belt and holster known as a 'Sam Browne'. Never having used weapons of any kind I had to be taught to shoot, which involved a trip to the RAF firing range where I was shown how to load the gun and then told to "get on with it". In front of me was a moving target with the outline of a man, which I blasted away at with some success.

While writing the above I am reminded of learning how to use my forward-firing gun when first becoming a Blenheim pilot. The ground gunnery officer had instructed me to fly up and shoot at a 'drogue' which was being towed by another plane, so I did, but upon landing and being shown the target I saw that it had no bullet holes in it at all. It came as no surprise, therefore, when I was told to go up again. This time I was determined to make some hits, but I flew so close to the drogue that I severed its metal cable with my bullets, resulting in the target being lost forever. It was a great relief when I landed to discover that the officer in charge of the range had a sense of humour. Laughing at my over-enthusiasm he gave me maximum marks.

Fortunately I never had to fire my service revolver in anger and unless I was on operations over enemy-occupied territory it was carefully stored in my locker. After five years in the service I was whisked away to sickbay with a suspected attack of food poisoning, but following various tests the diagnosis of a gastric ulcer was made. X-rays revealed a scar, which indicated that the ulcer had healed, so I was told that after seven days sick leave I would be able to return to my Squadron. Delighted by this news I celebrated my last morning in sickbay with kippers for breakfast, which I loved. Oh dear! As I was preparing to leave I was gripped by the most excruciating pains in the stomach, so severe, in fact, that an ambulance was summoned to take me, with lights flashing and bells ringing, to Shrewsbury General Hospital. Sadly, the ongoing effects of the gastric ulcer resulted in my ultimately being invalided out of the Royal Air Force.

During this dramatic time my revolver and personal kit disappeared from my locker, a situation which later came back to haunt me in the form of seemingly endless statements to be written. At last, however, the powers-that-be accepted the fact that my revolver must have been stolen during my stay in hospital, absolving me from any guilt.

Meanwhile, on my medical ward my fellow invalids and I were awaiting test results and became rather attached to one of the WAAF nurses, so upon discovering that it was her 21st birthday on the morrow, we managed to dress and hobble out to some shops to buy her a present. Once there we embarked on a long discussion as to what a beautiful 21-year-old girl would like, and not surprisingly plumped for a set of pretty underwear. After pooling our money and clothing coupons we entered the lingerie department of a large department store and upon being faced with rails of frilly undies, realised that we had no idea of her size. Then one of our group had the bright idea of asking all the female assistants to line up so that we could choose which one was closest in build to our 'birthday girl'. This led to much fun and laughter, but the result was a complete success, both in providing us with an enjoyable break from the hospital routine and in giving our favourite nurse a present which she really treasured.

Serving in The Home Guard

In 1939, following the declaration of war, everyone expected it to be a similar affair to the First World War, with a predominance of trench warfare. For several months there was a period of inactivity combined with a resigned anticipation, which became known as the 'Phoney War'. During this time young men like myself had not been taking hostilities very seriously, but suddenly the Germans began employing tactics they had used in the Spanish Civil War. These involved using vast numbers of aircraft, with tanks attacking along narrow fronts, striking deep into Holland, Belgium and Norway to capture vast areas of Allied territory, a manoeuvre which became known as the 'blitzkrieg'.

I was with my parents and brother at a holiday camp in Bognor Regis when news reached the British public that the Germans had broken through the supposedly impregnable Maginot Line of fortresses defending the French border. Within a few days France, Belgium, Holland, Denmark and Norway had all capitulated, leaving the UK to stand alone. It was then that Neville Chamberlain resigned as Prime Minister, handing over to Winston Churchill, who immediately appeared to stiffen the resolve of the government to fight on, a seemingly impossible task, as by then the Italians had sized up the situation and decided to join forces with the Germans.

The invasion of France by Germany and its capitulation filled me and most young people of my generation with the desire to 'do our bit'. Enough was enough, we decided, we had to do something, and quickly, if we did not want to become part of the German Third Reich. Straight after my family holiday, therefore, I volunteered for the Home Guard while awaiting the result of my application to train as a pilot with the RAF. I could have joined the army immediately, but two of my boyhood ambitions had been 1) to fly an aeroplane and 2) to drive a railway engine – both of which were to be fulfilled during my years in the RAF.

The Home Guard had been recently re-named, having been known previously as the Local Defence Volunteers (LDV). There was no uniform, just an armband with 'HG' on it. Once or twice a week about 20 or 30 of us would assemble in the local Boy Scouts Hall – a motley bunch which included those, like myself, who had recently left school and some recently retired veterans of the First World War. We learned discipline as a team and the importance of drill, so marching and PT formed a large part of our evening activities. There were lectures also, on subjects such as "using a radiotelephone" (which we did not possess) and "confronting the enemy".

On my first exercise concerning the latter I was on Home Guard duty with instructions to challenge anyone roaming on foot after midnight and to inspect their identity card. Feeling useful and important I was therefore pleased when someone approached through the pitch darkness of the blackout.

"Halt! Friend or foe?" I demanded, with all the air of authority I could muster, only to realise with embarrassment that I had no torch with which to check the man's ID. Fortunately, he was a 'friend' rather than a 'foe' and good-naturedly struck a match for me to check his papers. Rather bashfully I thanked him and hoped that the captain (our boss) would not come to learn of my carelessness.

Years later when *Dads Army* was shown on television I was sure that the Captain Mainwaring character had been modelled on our own captain, a short, fat, pompous little man who had retired from the regular Army and even carried a swagger stick, which he would tap against his trouser legs for affect. All in all, however, I enjoyed my spell in the Home Guard, but nevertheless was delighted to receive orders to report to RAF Uxbridge for a medical and assessment. Along with my peers, I wanted to put my training to good use and fight for my country.

Later, as RAF flying crews, our opinion of Germans in general tended to be rather muted compared to that of civilians, many of whom had suffered great personal losses, with homes destroyed and family members killed by enemy bombs. There was no doubt that as a result of air raid activities on both sides the civilian populations of the United Kingdom and Germany felt extremely anti-German or anti-British, as the case may have been, especially when forced to remain cooped up in air raid shelters for hours on end. For us, it was a different matter because in the RAF we viewed our German counterparts as opponents whom we respected, and they in turn respected us, for whichever side a chap was on he had a job to do to the best of his ability – i.e. that of defending his homeland.

Thus, with the bombing of Dresden, for example, in spite of it being razed to the ground, we had no strong feelings of sympathy or remorse; for us it was simply retaliation for what the Germans had been doing to our people.

Concerning the fate of the Jews, many of us in the services did not learn the full story of the horrors of the Holocaust until after the war was over. However, long before the armistice, news must have been trickling through, because I clearly recall the frustration and anger of my Jewish friends in London. Every time I saw them when on leave they would voice more and more urgent entreaties to me and my fellow pilots to "bomb as many military and civilian targets over there as you can and kill as many Jerries as possible". Such is war...

Religious Types

As far as religious beliefs were concerned, members of 114 Squadron differed enormously, from those who prayed regularly, and attended church two or three times every Sunday, to those, like myself, who remained totally fatalistic and were convinced that it was only a matter of luck as to whether or not one survived.

The latter group went on church parades because they were obligatory; dressed in our best uniforms we would march through town to the church and back – one of the few occasions when we had the company of our celebrated group Captain, the Earl of Bandon.

Whilst on the Squadron we had a padre who I remember well, no doubt because he was one of the most avid gamblers I have ever met. Unfortunately, he was also a cheat. During our impromptu card games he would use every sharp practice in the book and he and his partner somehow always managed to walk away with the cash.

It was not long before we cottoned on to our padre's duplicity, however, and thereafter we all kept a close eye on him whenever we played cards.

Being a good-natured group we did not bear grudges though, and one day when I mentioned to our padre that I sometimes went to watch greyhound racing whilst on leave he asked if he could join me.

Upon arriving at the stadium we found two queues, one for service personnel and one for civilians. We joined the former and the padre felt it would be prudent to remove the insignia from his lapels whilst he was waiting.

At last we arrived at the front of the queue, where military policeman studied our papers, with photographs attached, noticing that my companion's lapel badges had been removed.

"Not a very good likeness is it sir?" was his only comment.

In spite of my rather lukewarm feelings on religion and a certain padre, I have always felt a great deal of respect for the Salvation Army, both during the war and ever since...

Prior to the start of World War II all our aeroplanes had been kept together in hangars, but when hostilities commenced they were scattered as far apart as possible so that should the enemy bomb the airfield he would never hit more than one or two – a practice known as "dispersal".

I remember vividly one occasion when we had been posted to a remote locality and the mess was some distance from dispersals, which meant that our ground crews had to work in a sort of no-man's-land, in all weathers, for hours on end.

It was then such a comforting sight to see the good old 'Sally Ann' wagon rolling up to the airstrip, whereupon they would dole out "a cup of tea and a wad" to all the ground crews (and we airman also, if time permitted).

"Lack of Moral Fibre"

Cowardice in the face of the enemy was always referred to as "lack of moral fibre" or "LMF" and was taken very seriously. Aircrews who failed to reach their targets or returned to base early with technical problems would come under scrutiny.

This had not really registered with me until one day during one of our bombing raids over France...

We had just dropped our bomb-load when suddenly the port engine began backfiring, sending great showers of sparks gushing out before finally packing up altogether. As we were heading for home I was very relieved, however, when the faulty engine explosively restarted of its own accord, allowing me to make a normal landing.

Upon being debriefed I reported that we had experienced engine trouble over the target. The very next day our engineering officer approached me, saying: "You were quite right about your port engine, Shack, one of the valves was sticking."

Having completed 20 operations at the time I was rather taken aback that anyone should query my integrity, or indeed even hint that I might not be telling the truth. Later, I discussed the matter with a fellow pilot, who just shrugged, saying: "He probably thought you were suffering from a touch of LMF, old chap."

Not long after the above incident my crew and I were alerted to the fact that one of the crews – who had been on rest at OTU and were now coming back on operations for a second tour – always returned to base at the exact time it would have taken to fly directly to the target and back. Nothing was ever said, but we all thought that such "coincidences" were highly suspicious.

There were some occasions, of course, when cases of LMF were proved beyond any shadow of a doubt, such as when one of our crews forgot to turn off their IFF.[6] Due to this oversight their aircraft was plotted on a radar screen at Group HQ and was observed to be flying in circles over the North Sea instead of proceeding to its target in Germany. Its bombs were dumped at sea before returning home.

Whenever a case of LMF was discovered, that particular crew quietly disappeared to be posted on to a non-operational squadron.

---

[6] Identification Friend or Foe, a device which enabled our planes to be identified as friendly by our own UK radar installations, but which was supposed to be switched off as soon as one was out of UK airspace.

Such cases were never discussed because if word of such events were ever to reach the ears of our own trusting British public, morale would have been severely smitten.

As far as the UK public were concerned their RAF boys were fearless heroes, which was not always the case, of course.

However, I can speak for most of my fellow pilots when I say that if some chaps were not scared sometimes then they must have had a total lack of imagination.

Back to Civilian Life

Following five years in the Royal Air Force I was invalided out and returned to work in the family wholesale fruit and vegetable business, which I thoroughly enjoyed. My chosen role was that of buyer, which involved walking for miles around Spitalfields market between five o'clock and eight o'clock each morning. Despite the earliness of the hour it was a fun place to be, filled with memorable characters, most of whom had a great sense of humour. Not surprisingly, therefore, practical jokes were commonplace, one being to put a handful of burning wood-wool (used for packing fruit) into a fellow's trilby hat, then to point out the victim to somebody else, whose hat had been given a similar treatment. The second chap would laugh at the burning hat, unaware that his own trilby now had flames coming from it, and the two men with burning headgear would be pointing at each other and laughing, each thinking that the other was the butt of the joke. Such capers provided tremendous amusement for everybody around and offered welcome light relief during those wartime years.

Apart from loading and unloading lorries, the market porters would also do the fruit and vegetable displays. Being experts, they would often go through five or ten bushels of apples, for example, in order to find those of the right colour, size and shape to tempt buyers like myself. However, experience had taught us that what was on display was generally untypical of what was being sold, and one would always ask to see inside the sacks or boxes if possible, delving deeply to extract a sample from the bottom layer before buying.

On the salad stands were large coppers steaming with boiling beetroot, while other stands did a roaring trade in freshly cooked eels for hungry workers. Not for me though, as in spite of being a Londoner, eels were a dish which I never found tempting. A full English cooked breakfast was another matter, however, and between nine and ten, when all the early buying was finished, my friends and I would descend upon Spitalfields 'greasy spoon' café for a delicious fry-up.

Fruit auctions were held on Mondays and Wednesdays at the London Fruit Exchange in Spitalfields Market and on Tuesdays and Thursdays at the Borough Market near London Bridge. They began after we had finished breakfast and were always worth attending for the entertainment value alone. All the auctioneers had their idiosyncrasies, one for example being so fast it was like listening to expert Morse Code. He had to have a team of six men noting down what had been bought by whom, as it was not uncommon for him to go through 500 lots in less than half an hour.

Another auctioneer used to go in for what we referred to as "trotting" – i.e. he would take imaginary bids from the radiators, for instance. If challenged, he would cheerfully say: "then let us go back to the beginning" or "as nobody wants any of this, I have got better things to do than stand in front of you lot wasting my time!", which was the cue for someone to shout: "Hang on a minute, I have not travelled all the way from Ireland (or Scotland, for instance, as buyers came from all over the UK) for nothing!" Then the auctioneer would start all over again, of course...

During the war, cabbages and carrots were not price-controlled and were plentiful, so were used by market salesmen as a bargaining tool against items such as English apples, which were price-controlled and which during the winter months became scarce. For example, if I bought 50 sacks of carrots in December I could expect to be offered 10 boxes of apples, which were then in short supply... conditions of sale were illegal, however, so were not discussed, but I and the other buyers knew that if we did not purchase items which were plentiful we would discover that the apples we really wanted would all have been 'sold'. However, if we returned to the same salesmen later to buy carrots, for instance, he might say: "wait a minute, I believe I *have* got a few apples left, I will just go and check..."

The war years meant that there were no private imports of foreign fruits; supplies were all government-controlled.

Californian oranges were the only citrus fruit imports available most of the time and these were on children's ration books only. On one occasion, however, there was a very rare overnight frost in California which virtually wiped out the orange crops, causing the price to double and treble overnight. Our UK buyers then said that they would take grapefruit instead, as our ships were empty and already in the States waiting to be loaded, added to which, grapefruit, at that time, were extremely cheap. Thus my family business received an unexpected allocation of grapefruit, which most English housewives had never seen, let alone tasted, so I got the job of giving lessons to our customers on how to prepare and eat them.

In those days grapefruit were very sour and full of pips, so my advice was for them to be halved, cut into segments, covered with sugar and allowed to stand overnight. My final words being: "and do not forget to spit out the pips!" Needless to say, most people only bought our English apples and pears until oranges returned.

With the war years came a severe shortage of manpower, many able-bodied males being away fighting for their country, thus my parents employed residents from a nearby psychiatric hospital, which allowed its non-dangerous patients to go out to work each day. In exchange for a small wage we gave these chaps simple tasks to perform and they enjoyed the freedom and independence which this arrangement offered them, while we in turn became quite fond of our 'special' employees, some of whom were unforgettable characters.

For instance, there was one man called Harry who, given a better start in life could have become one of our country's successful entrepreneur millionaires I am sure, as he seemed to have a never-ending supply of money-making ideas. For example, on his way to work each morning he would stop at all the pubs en route to collect cigarette ends from their ashtrays. He would then pop into the lavatory and use the shiny toilet paper to wrap the old tobacco and roll cigarettes. Appearing in our office he would offer them for sale, and as cigarettes were then in short supply he had plenty of eager customers.

Another of our friend's moneymaking projects was to collect dripping from any roast dinners prepared by my mother and her friends. Then, helping himself to crusts of bread that nobody wanted, he would make 'door-stop' dripping sand-wiches which he sold to fellow patients at the psychiatric hospital as 'tasty snacks'. I never discovered why our Harry lived where he did, but I shall always remember him as one of England's delightful eccentrics.

As I have already mentioned, the war was still on when I was invalided out of the RAF and whether it was due to relief at having me home safely or to show me off in my smart RAF officer's uniform, I was not sure, but my parents suddenly took me for a round of visits to our London relatives.

My father drove us in his pre-war, two-door saloon and upon arriving home afterwards my mother got out, forgetting that I would be following from the rear seat. Without a backward glance she slammed the door shut just as I was following with my head down. Pre-war cars were built to last and were made of solid stuff, so the next thing I remember was being flat on my back on the rear seat seeing stars, with my father shouting, "Get up you bloody fool, can't you see you're frightening your mother?"

With a handkerchief I tried to staunch the heavy bleeding from a large gash in my head while giving my parents a rather crooked but what I hoped was a reassuring and encouraging smile. Then, in a dazed voice I told them that I was perfectly all right. By this time my mother was hysterical with worry, fearing that her 'little boy' (now well into his twenties, I may say) was about to bleed to death before her very eyes. She insisted that I be taken to our family doctor, who spent only a few minutes dressing my wound, but then spent half an hour treating my mother for shock.

Luckily, neither of us suffered any permanent ill effects, but I often wonder how she would have reacted if she had known about, let alone seen, the injuries I sustained during my flying career.

VE Night

During the months following my demob and prior to the end of the war, Lord Haw Haw's pompous, confident announcements would still erupt from our crackling wireless set, telling us that it was only a matter of time before Germany was the glorious victor. However, along with most of my compatriots I felt sure of Britain's imminent success, one reason being that the RAF was by then flying over Germany and occupied Europe with very little enemy opposition. At the same time our Allied armies were heading steadfastly across the Third Reich en route to Berlin, while the Royal Navy was more in control of the seas than at any other time during the hostilities, the only resistance being German U-boats, which were now being sunk with gratifying accuracy.

However, right until our Allied troops swept through France into Germany, Hitler was using occupied French bases from which to launch Germany's 'V' weapons, which were his response to Britain's bombing raids on German cities.

By that time, when the war was coming to an end, there were very few raids over England by the Luftwaffe, who were hardly visible at all. Instead we were bombarded by Hitler's projectiles: the V1 flying bomb, also known as the 'doodlebug' and the V2 rocket, which was the first true missile. The former were like miniature aeroplanes and when they came overhead we knew what was about to happen because their engines would cut out, followed by a deafening silence while we awaited the inevitable explosion. The V2s, however, were larger and being rockets gave no warning whatsoever. Suddenly there would be a huge explosion and a house would be blown to pieces before our eyes, which was a terrifying experience. One of the most frightening things I saw at that time was when a V2 rocket exploded right in the middle of Balham High Street, blowing a hole right down to the Tube Station underneath, from which protruded the top of a double-decker bus.

Thus VE Day in May 1945, when the war in Europe was won, actually seemed rather a subdued occasion for us Londoners, no doubt because our nerves were well and truly shattered by the 'V' weapons, combined with sadness due to the loss of so many friends.

VE night, however, was a different story, as the lights of London went on again for the first time in nearly six years. Celebrations were going on everywhere, of course, but not being a drinking man myself I did not make for the nearest pub and was content to walk with my parents and other members of my family through our capital's bright, busy, bustling and once more unthreatened streets, finishing up with a jolly communal barbecue.

Perhaps another reason for the feeling of a sort of post-war anticlimax was that rationing then became even more severe, with allowances of meat and petrol, for example, being even less than when we were fighting the enemy. For several years following VE Day, in fact, Britain suffered much austerity, and it was some time before we could really sigh with relief and look towards a better future.

However, the war years had taught me personally that life's greatest pleasures could in fact be free, with simple occupations costing nothing yet affording great enjoyment. An example of this came when I first went into the air force and was at a receiving wing in Torquay.

As described earlier, most days were taken up with getting one's inoculations, learning drill and having lectures on such diverse subjects as aerodynamics, Morse code, and how to avoid VD.

When we did get some time off a group of us would go for walks over the nearby Babbacombe cliffs, our pockets stuffed with bread crusts taken from the mess waste-bin. Heading for the cliffs' edge we would throw our bread high into the air above the sea, and be thrilled as the seagulls swooped down into the sheer drop below, snatching their prize just before it hit the white-capped waves. Then, spreading their wings, they would climb back up into the sky with bread-filled beaks and we would marvel at the aerodynamics of birds, spending many happy hours together, which cost us nothing.

If we were lucky, and had some spare time, we would scramble down the cliffs for a refreshing swim, then our enjoyment would be complete, while making it extra special for us was the fact that due to the threat of invasion, the beaches were a restricted zone to all except servicemen. Thus we swam from our own 'private' beach, feeling privileged and rather like millionaires at leisure.

Later, when I was fully-fledged pilot and on my squadron at West Raynham, those of us who had returned from night Ops had the opportunity to partake of another of life's simple pleasures. The season was autumn and perfect for mushroom picking, so we would always make a detour through some fields when going back to the mess. Soon our flying helmets were filled with enormous mushrooms, which would appear later as a free and delicious addition to our cooked breakfasts.

There is no doubt that fighting for one's country and having to accept death as an occupational hazard helped one to sort out one's priorities. For example, I appreciated just being alive and every time I was able to enjoy another leave I always counted my blessings. It was because of this that I filled my post-war free time doing charity work, something I felt privileged to be able to do, and my way of saying 'thanks' for having been spared.

Some years after VE Day I was watching the November 11th March Past with a friend and remember saying: "In retrospect, I feel rather relieved at not having won any 'gongs' whilst in the RAF, because I'm sure that they would have been posthumous!"

Remembering My Crew

Earlier in this account I mentioned the crew with whom I shared all my operational duties whilst on 114 Squadron. My wireless operator/air-gunner was Sgt Bill Kennedy, a Scot from Stirlingshire, while Sgt Frank Eyres was my navigator/bomb-aimer and hailed from Southport in Lancashire. We all got on well together, and although after the war I never learned the whereabouts of Frank, Bill Kennedy and I corresponded regularly.

During the course of our time together in the RAF we shared many exciting and at times hair-raising experiences, such as when we went out on low-level shipping 'beats'...

Intelligence would report a convoy of enemy ships within a certain area and we were then ordered to fly in formations of three and head for the map coordinates which had been given. When we arrived over the sea we would all make a right-hand turn and fly at 180 miles per hour for three minutes, bombing any German shipping that we saw below us. Afterwards there was no question of hanging around, as we were within sight of the German coastline, from where fighters were on standby to come and attack us.

One day, we were on a shipping beat off the Danish coast when suddenly, emerging from the clouds, we found ourselves almost on top of a small convoy of German merchant ships with an escort of flak ships and destroyers. Taking the safest way out, we dropped down to wave height and flew between the enemy vessels, so that they were unable to fire at us without risking hitting each other. Even so, just as we came to the end of the convoy and were ascending as rapidly as possible to a safe distance, some flak burst close to our plane and shrapnel from the explosion penetrated the fuselage.

"Is every one okay?" I enquired, to which Frank replied, "My seat has been shot away!"

"Well sit on the floor, then," I told him, to which Frank yelled (in a rather high-pitched voice, I might add) "Not *the* seat, *my* seat!" and I realised that a piece of shrapnel had hit the unfortunate Frank in the rear end, causing a painful and somewhat embarrassing wound.

During night-time bombing raids, we were never escorted by fighters, as in the dark they could not have seen us and (hopefully) neither could the enemy. However, when doing daylight bombing sorties over Germany, France, Belgium or Holland we would be escorted by fighters such as Spitfires, Hurricanes and Whirlwinds, which left us en route as they did not have the range (fuel-wise) to accompany us as far as the target. On our homeward leg it was with a great sense of relief that we saw the fighters again, especially when our planes had been damaged during the raids.

It was extremely important, of course, for us to recognise the oncoming fighter aircraft as being British, and because most pilots and navigators were not too good at quickly identifying aeroplanes, that task inevitably fell on the shoulders of one's air gunner, in our case, Bill. We did have a wee handicap, however, as when our Scottish friend was excitedly naming the rapidly-approaching fighters his Scottish accent became an incomprehensible gabble of broad dialect. When accused of this later, Bill would vehemently deny it, but some years afterwards he was caught out by none other than the BBC...

Having been stationed in England for several years he was sure that the rough edges of his Scottish brogue had long since disappeared and was pleased that his crew was chosen when the BBC wanted to make a recording on board a Lancaster during an actual bombing raid. Following a successful operation the crew were treated to a replay of the recording and at one point, the pilot asked Bill (the tailgunner) to report on enemy night-fighter activity.

Describing it to me later Bill said, "To my horror my reply included things like "Och aye, everything's fine doon here" and my fondly-held illusion of having a refined Scottish accent was lost for ever!"

Much less dramatic than our bombing raids were the air sea rescue searches, which took place when our Squadron Commander received word from other squadrons that a plane had recently ditched over the sea. We were then sent out with specific map references to conduct an ASR search, which entailed six or seven hours of monotonous flying over the waves, straining our eyes to look for a dinghy, never daring to relax for a second as we solemnly thought, "there but for the grace of God go I". If a dinghy was spotted, our navigator Frank would radio back to HQ with the craft's position and an ASR launch would come out to pick up the crew.

A rather more memorable and somewhat risky search was described in my account of the *Scharnhorst* and *Gneisenau* incident – an operation which made a lasting and vivid impression on my crew and I. The famous channel breakout on 12th of February 1942 involved these two German battle-ships (sister ships of the notorious *Bismarck* and *Tirpitz*). The German Navy had taken advantage of very poor weather conditions for the vessels to re-enter the Atlantic Ocean after refit work in Brest Harbour, and only too aware of the havoc these ships would wreak upon our merchant fleet and the ships of the Royal Navy, Churchill ordered a full-scale search. This involved every available aircraft, one of those planes being the Bristol Blenheim crewed by Bill, Frank and myself. Due to low cloud, visibility was poor, so I decided to dive through it to get a better look. Later my air gunner Bill gave me his account of what followed:

> *"I was in the upper turret and suddenly all I could see from my far left to far right was this huge bloody ship, flashing with lights. It was like Blackpool's illuminations! Every gun was firing at us and it sparkled from end to end. At this point two huge black things went rushing past and I realised they had fired their main guns at us. Somebody shouted, 'Get the hell out of here!' or words to that effect, so Gordon put the plane into an immediate climb to the safety of the clouds, hotly pursued for a short period by two or three Messerschmitt 109s. This was our first and last encounter with the two enemy ships."*

Back in the mess that evening I saw Bill's flight logbook for February 12th and smiled. Very soberly it read: "Day Ops, *Scharnhorst* & *Gneisenau*. Did not bomb." However, over a few drinks my friend confided: "I really thought we had bought it Gordon, but as usual, your strong arms with their potato-sack carrying muscles pulled our old kite round and up and didn't let us down!"

After the war, when pressed by my friends and family to recall some of my most hair-raising incidents when on Ops the question "were you afraid?" would often crop up. "Yes, of course," I truthfully replied, "but it would have taken more courage for me to have admitted that I was not only afraid but at times terrified than to just press on regardless." In fact, it was always easy to put on a brave face in the company of colleagues. The people I really admire were those in the resistance or our spies acting alone behind enemy lines, knowing that should they be caught there could only be one outcome...

I have already written on the subject of mess parties, but I really must mention here that Bill Kennedy's Hogmanay celebrations were a tribute to every one of his Scottish ancestors. Along with fellow Scots, Bill would think nothing of dragging an engine crane into the centre of the hangar, up which the most inebriated of the chaps would proceed to climb. They would then be pelted with beer bottles by those on the ground, the trick being to dodge the missiles and descend unscathed. By this point in the proceedings, however, I would have gone to bed, being neither a lover of alcohol or the horseplay it provokes.

However, Bill was a witty, amusing character, whose company I enjoyed, not only in the air but in the mess also and one evening I watched as he was challenged about the Scots' reputation as whisky drinkers. His reply was: "If you buy it, I will drink it!" Thus many whiskies were bought, and he duly drank them all, even managing to remain standing. After a long session he put on his cap, bade me and his co-drinkers goodnight, and walked (not staggered) happily back to his billet, where (he confided to me later) he went to the lavatory, put two fingers down his throat and promptly brought up all the whisky consumed during the evening. Many with sore heads were surprised to see him looking very well the next morning, whilst the (undeserved!) drinking reputation of the Scots remained intact.

My memory fails me with regard to Frank Eyres, but I do recall that he also had a good sense of humour. One morning upon surveying our sloppy formation flying following a mess party he exclaimed with a grin: "Here go the Blenheim boys again, flying in their inter-counties formation!"

In 1998, I received the sad news of Bill's death from Bill Kennedy Jr, who sent me a copy of his father's obituary, which I treasure to this day. It reads:

"William Kennedy, who has died at the age of 77 was a major figure in secondary education in Scotland, who also had a distinguished war record. He was born in Greenock, a second son of a pit electrician but the family moved to Fallon in Stirlingshire, and after attending Stirling High School he joined the Post Office, working initially as a sorting clerk and later as a trainee telegraphist.

With the outbreak of war, he volunteered for service with the Royal Air Force and began his training as a wireless operator/air gunner, flying as part of the three-man crew of the Blenheim light bomber, as a sergeant. He later transferred to No.49 Squadron, flying Lancasters from RAF Syerston in Nottinghamshire. During this period he was promoted to the rank of Flight Lieutenant and flew two tours of operations over Germany as a rear gunner, the notorious 'Tail-End Charlie', whose vigilance provided the only defence against the constant threat from enemy night-fighters.

At a time when the life expectancy of the average Lancaster crew might be counted in days he remained in the thick of the action and somehow survived, being awarded the DFC for his conduct. In addition to flying, he acted as an air gunnery instructor, teaching Australian bomber crews.

When peace returned, he took advantage of the grants available to ex-servicemen and began studying English and history at Edinburgh University. It was there that he met his future wife, Elsa, with whom he went on teacher training at Moray House College of Education.

For over 10 years, he taught in schools throughout Stirlingshire and in 1964 he became rector of Woodlands Junior Secondary in Falkirk. He transformed it into a viable fifth-year school, presenting pupils for SCE Highers, which it had never previously done.

In 1973 he became Rector of Balfron High School, at that time a school of poor reputation, which was regarded as having fallen on hard times. In the ensuing years he employed his wealth of experience to effect a complete turnaround and under his leadership the school achieved a fine academic reputation.

In 1981 ill-health forced his retirement but he continued to follow his great loves of English and Poetry through the works of Shakespeare and particularly Robert Burns, on whose works he was an authority.

William Kennedy was predeceased by his wife and is survived by three daughters and two sons."

As I have previously written, neither Frank, Bill nor I ever expected to see our next leave, the average life expectancy of bomber crews being so short, yet Bill and I were blessed with having survived for many years after the war – years during which I endeavoured, by helping my fellow men, to say 'thank you' for having been spared.

When I reflect upon what dear Bill achieved during his own post-war years there is no doubt in my mind that he was busily doing the same.

~ END ~

The crew of Blenheim 'L' for London serving with 114 Squadron, West Raynham, 1941: (left to right) Gordon Shackleton (pilot), Frank Eyres (navigator/bomb-aimer) and Bill Kennedy (wireless operator/air gunner).

Gordon and Frank in the cockpit of Blenheim 'L' for London.

King George V and Queen Elizabeth visit West Raynham. Group Captain The Earl of Bandon (Station Commander) is in the foreground.

The tail wheel of 'L' for London over Herdla aerodrome, Norway, taken by the automatic camera triggered upon bomb release. Note the Messerschmitt 109 on the move down on the runway -- shortly afterwards it fell into a crater which appeared suddenly, just in front of it.

928746

Form 2171

ROYAL AIR FORCE VOLUNTEER RESERVE
(IN EMERGENCY)

FORM OF APPLICATION

for enlistment for aircraft crew duties, i.e., pilot, air observer, air gunner, or wireless operator-air gunner.

Please read these notes before completing the form :—

(a) All questions must be answered in candidate's own handwriting; it is not sufficient to leave the space for reply blank or to insert a dash. Incorrect answers may prejudice a candidate's chance of selection.

(b) When completed this form should be attached to the applicant's attestation form.

(c) The submission by a candidate of false or falsified documents or certificates in connection with his application may render the candidate liable to prosecution.

A. Particulars to be furnished by all candidates :—

(i) Surname (in capitals) .. *SHACKLETON*

(ii) Christian Names (in full, in capitals) .. .. *GORDON LESLIE*

(iii) Present address for correspondence, and date to which it holds good .. *151 Seaforth Gnds Stoneleigh, Ewell. Surrey*

B. State duties for which volunteering, *i.e.*, pilot, air observer, air gunner, or wireless operator-air gunner (to be given in order of preference). *Pilot. air observer. W0/A G.*

C.	Names and addresses of Schools and Colleges.	Period of Education.	
		From	To
(i) Give particulars opposite of the schools and colleges at which you were educated from the age of 12.	*Bec Secondary School*	*1934*	*1937*
	Bonneville Rd. Clapham.	*1933*	*1934*

[P.T.O.

Gordon's application to join the RAFVR in 1940 (continued on following pages)

(ii) Have you sat for the matriculation examination or for a school certificate? If so, give particulars opposite.

Name of examining body......No......

Description of certificate......No......

Date of examination......No......

Was certificate obtained?......No......

Subjects passed in......No......

Subjects failed in......

Subjects (if any) in which "credit" or "distinction" was obtained

(iii) Have you sat for any other educational examination? If so, give particulars opposite.

Name of examining body......No......

Description of examination......No......

Date of examination......No......

Was examination passed?......No......

Particulars of subjects passed in......No......

(iv) Give particulars of further education undertaken since leaving school.

Night-school. (6 months.)
Private lessons in Mathematics (1 month)

D. Occupation since leaving school or college, giving names, full addresses and business of employers, dates between which employed, nature of work (in detail) on which engaged and cause of leaving. (Details to be entered on separate sheet, if necessary.)

Salesman (Wholesale). Austin's (Fruiterers) Ltd
East. St. Epsom.
Since leaving school. 1937.

E. I hereby certify the details hereon to be correct.

Date......5th June 1940......G. S. Shackleton......
(Usual signature of candidate.)

F. Decision of No.   R.A.F. (Aviation Candidates) Selection Board.

Accepted - Pilot

Date......June 5/40......

Signature of Chairman of Board......W. Tringhall......

(C32004) 10,000 8/39

~ 162 ~

17. Have you ever sat for any other education or professional examination? If so, give the following particulars:- No
(i) Name of examining body .... N/A
(ii) Description of examination .... N/A
(iii) Date of examination .... N/A
(iv) as examination passed .... N/A
(v) Particulars of subjects passed in . N/A

18. Give particulars, with dates, of further education undertaken since leaving school. Name and address of educational establishment or tutor should be stated, subjects taken and whether whole or part time tuition.

TOOTING NIGHT SCHOOL. OCT 1937. MORSE 1938.ENGLISH, MACHINING
MR. FRAZER, 22 SPRINGFIELD DRIVE EWELL. 1.5.40 - 25.7.40
ADVANCED MATHEMATICS. PART TIME

19. Have you ever previously served in any branch of H.M. Forces (Regular, reserve or auxiliary) or in an officers' training corps/unit? If so, give the following particulars:- No

(i) Unit (stating whether regular, auxiliary, territorial, reserve etc). .... N/A

(ii) Date of joining .... N/A
(iii) Rank or grade .... N/A
(iv) Regimental, official or service number .. N/A
(v) Cause of leaving .... N/A
(vi) Have you obtained an O.T.C certificate? If so, give particulars .... N/A

I HEREBY CERTIFY THE DETAILS STATED HEREIN TO BE CORRECT.
Airman's signature and date ... G. L. Shackleton
9. 1. 42.

B. MEDICAL OFFICER'S CERTIFICATE.

The airman named above is considered, after medical examination and scrutiny of available medical records, to be FIT/UNFIT for presentation to a medical board for final examination as is his fitness for appointment to a commission.
having had a medical board on 5/1/42
Signature and date .. A. Turnbull F/o .. 9/1/42

C. REMARKS OF BRANCH COMMANDER.

Sgt. Shackleton has been in the Squadron since August 1941 and has shown himself a really reliable pilot. His qualities of steadiness and keenness make him an example to the rest of the squadron. I consider that this N.C.O. is capable of performing the duties of an officer, and has the necessary personal qualities.
Mandan   S/Ldr
R.A.F. STATION, WEST RAYNHAM.

D. REMARKS OF A.O.C.

I concur in the remarks in para C and recommend this NCO. for a commission.

Signature ...... A.VH.
Signature to be reproduced in Block Capitals ...... A. LEES

Command or Group and Place
Headquarters, No.2 Group, Huntingdon.   Date 15. 4. 42.

PART IV

INFORMATION SUPPLIED BY RECRUIT

Name and address of Next-of-Kin.......... Mr W. Shackleton   151 Seaforth Gardens,
.....Stoneleigh....Epsom....Surrey,... Relationship....Self.....

Name, Address and Relationship of Persons to be informed of Casualties (if not Next-of-Kin)

....

....

Particulars as to Marriage

Christian and Surname of Woman to whom married and whether Spinster or Widow.	Place and Date of Marriage.	Postal Address.

Particulars as to Children

Christian Names.	Date and Place of Birth.

UNEMPLOYMENT INSURANCE BRANCH.......Epsom.......

BOOK NUMBER.......16213.......

PART V

CERTIFICATE OF APPROVING OFFICER

I certify that this Attestation of the above-named Recruit is correct and properly filled up, and that the required forms have been complied with.

Date.... - 6 JUN 1940 ....19 .

Place.................................. _For_ Officer i/c Records, Royal Air Force } Approving Officer.

(C35037) 180,000 7/39 T.S.4562

~ 164 ~

I, Gordon Leslie Shackleton ......do solemnly declare that the foregoing answers made by me to the foregoing questions are true, and that I am willing to fulfil the engagements made.

SIGNATURE OF RECRUIT... G. L. Shackleton

SIGNATURE OF WITNESS... E Harvey Sp -

OATH TO BE TAKEN BY RECRUIT ON ATTESTATION

I, Gordon Leslie Shackleton ......swear by Almighty God that I will be faithful and bear true allegiance to His Majesty King George the Sixth, His Heirs and Successors, and that I will, as in duty bound, honestly and faithfully defend His Majesty, His Heirs and Successors, in Person, Crown and Dignity against all enemies, and will observe and obey all orders of His Majesty, His Heirs and Successors, and of the Air Officers and Officers set over me. So help me God.

CERTIFICATE OF ATTESTING OFFICER

The Recruit above named was cautioned by me that if he wilfully or knowingly made any false answer to any of the foregoing questions, he would be liable to be punished as provided by the Air Force Act.

The foregoing questions were then read to the Recruit in my presence.

I have taken care that he understands each question, and that his answer to each question has been duly entered as replied to. He has been inspected by me, I consider him fit for service in the Royal Air Force Volunteer Reserve and due care has been exercised in his enlistment. The said Recruit has made and signed the Declaration and taken the Oath before me at UXBRIDGE, on this 5th day of June 19 40

Signature of Attesting Officer,

If any alteration is required on this page of the Attestation a Justice of the Peace or Attesting Officer should be requested to make it and initial the alteration as required by Section 80 (6), Air Force Act. The Recruit should, if he require it, receive a copy of the Declaration on Form No. 2168.

DECLARATION BY RECRUIT.

I _Gordon Leslie Shackleton_ fully understand :—

(i) The conditions of service in the Royal Air Force Volunteer Reserve, and that enlistment is for the duration of the present emergency.

(ii) I am being sent forward for enlistment, subject to my suitability, as

a6+/air crew

and that I will not be allowed to remuster to another trade.

(iii) That my pay will be :—

(a) 2s. per day, if I am enlisted as an Aircrafthand or Aircrafthand under training, and that if I undergo training I will not receive the R.A.F. pay of my trade until I have satisfactorily completed my instruction;

_or_

(b) the R.A.F. pay of my trade if I am enlisted as a skilled man ;

_or_

(c) as outlined in A.M. Pamphlet 96, if I am attested as Air Crew.

(iv) Rates of family allowances for married men.

(v) In the event of my attestation and my services not being immediately required, that I will be sent home on deferred service and that pay, and allowances (if applicable), will not commence until I am called up for full time service.

Signed _G. L. Shackleton_

Date _5th June 1940_

(*4461) Wt. 46967—4374 50,000 2/40 T.S. 700
(*4665—4461) Wt. 31407—4698 100,000 3/40 T.S. 700

The following pages contain a selection of entries from Gordon's flying log book, recording his flying training and the operations in which he took part during his tour of Ops on 114 Squadron in 1941-42.

PILOTS' FLYING LOG BOOKS ~ STANDARD ENTRIES.

1.   Air Experience.
1A. Familiarity with cockpit layout.
2.   Effect of controls.
3.   Taxying.
4.   Straight and level flying.
5.   Climbing, gliding and stalling.
6.   Medium turns.
7.   Taking off into wind.
8.   Powered approach and landing.
9.   Action in the event of fire) To be given on the ground.
9A. Abandoning an aircraft   )
10. First solo.
11. Steep turns.
12. Climbing turns.
13. Gliding approach and landing.
14. Low flying (with instructor only).
15. Precautionary landing.
         A. Half power.
         B. Full power.
16. Instrument flying.
17. Night flying.
18. Navigation.
19. Cross country test.
20. Formation.
21. Height test.

N.B. 1A, To be given to pupils in "mock up" cockpit or
      jacked up aircraft.

      9 and 9A. To be given on the ground.

1. This book is an official document and is the property of His Majesty's Government.

2. An accurate and detailed record is to be kept in the log of all flights undertaken by the individual to whom it relates.

3. Monthly flying will be analysed by aircraft types and inserted in red ink. The stamp will be inserted on the left-hand page appropriately aligned to the ruling.

4. The annual summary and assessment will be completed on Form 414 A and inserted in the appropriate page of the log. This form will also be used when a pilot is posted or attached to another unit for flying duties.

Year 1940		Aircraft		Pilot, or 1st Pilot	2nd Pilot, Pupil or Passenger	Duty (Including Results and Remarks)
Month	Date	Type	No.			
—	—	—	—	—	—	—— Totals Brought Forward
Oct.	1	Magister	R.1840	Sgt Jeffries	SELF	3. Taxying
						4. Straight and Level Flight
						5. Climbing Gliding and Stalling
"	1	Magister	R1840	Sgt Jeffries	SELF	3 Taxying
						4. Straight and Level Flight
						5 Climbing Gliding and Stalling
"	2	Magister	R1840	Sgt Jeffries	SELF	5. Climbing Gliding and Stalling
						6 Medium Turns
"	3	Magister	R1840	Sgt Jeffries	SELF	5. Climbing Gliding and Stalling
						6. Medium Turns
"	3	Magister	R1840	Sgt Jeffries	SELF	4. Straight and Level Flight
						5 Climbing Gliding and Stalling
						6. Medium Turns
"	4	Magister	R1840	Sgt Jeffries	SELF	6 Medium Turns
						7 Taking off into Wind
						8 Powered Approach and Landing
"	6	Magister	R1848	P/o Robinson	SELF	7 Taking off into Wind
						8 Powered Approach and Landing

GRAND TOTAL [Cols. (1) to (10)]
........5........Hrs....4.5........Mins.

Totals Carried Forward

~ 169 ~

YEAR 1940		AIRCRAFT		PILOT, OR 1ST PILOT	2ND PILOT, PUPIL OR PASSENGER	DUTY (INCLUDING RESULTS AND REMARKS)
MONTH	DATE	Type	No.			
—	—	—	—	—	—	Totals Brought Forward
Oct.	7	MAGISTER	R1851	P/O HAGGAR	SELF	10. SPINNING
''	10	MAGISTER	R1851	P/O HAGGAR	SELF	7 TAKING OFF INTO WIND 8. POWERED APPROACH AND LANDING
''	11	MAGISTER	R1840	Sgt JEFFRIES	SELF	7. TAKING OFF INTO WIND 8. POWERED APPROACH AND LANDING
''	12	MAGISTER	R1840	Sgt JEFFRIES	SELF	7 TAKING OFF INTO WIND 8 POWERED APPROACH AND LANDING 9 GLIDING APPROACH AND LANDING
''	12	MAGISTER	R1840	Sgt JEFFRIES	SELF	7 TAKING OFF INTO WIND 8 POWERED APPROACH AND LANDING
''	12	MAGISTER	R1840	Sgt JEFFRIES	SELF	7 TAKING OFF INTO WIND 8 POWERED APPROACH AND LANDING
''	13	MAGISTER	R1840	Sgt JEFFRIES	SELF	7 TAKING OFF INTO WIND 8. POWERED APPROACH AND LANDING
''	13	MAGISTER	R1840	F/Lt LINES	SELF	F/C TEST
''	13	MAGISTER	R1840	SELF	—	11 FIRST SOLO

GRAND TOTAL [Cols. (1) to (10)] ...12... Hrs. ...20... Mins.

TOTALS CARRIED FORWARD

First solo flight in a Magister on 13 October.

YEAR 1940		AIRCRAFT		PILOT, OR 1ST PILOT	2ND PILOT, PUPIL OR PASSENGER	DUTY (INCLUDING RESULTS AND REMARKS)
MONTH	DATE	Type	No.			
	—	—	—	—	—	— TOTALS BROUGHT FORWARD
Oct	13	MAGISTER	R1840	Sgt JEFFRIES	SELF	7. TAKING OFF INTO WIND
						8. POWERED APPROACH AND LANDING
..	13	MAGISTER	R1840	SELF	—	6 MEDIUM TURNS
						7 TAKING OFF INTO WIND
						8 POWERED APPROACH AND LANDING
	14	MAGISTER	R1840	Sgt JEFFRIES	SELF	7 TAKING OFF INTO WIND
						9 GLIDING APPROACH AND LANDING
	14	MAGISTER	R1840	SELF	—	7 TAKING OFF INTO WIND
						8 POWERED APPROACH AND LANDING
						9 GLIDING APPROACH AND LANDING
	14	MAGISTER	L8352	SELF	—	6 MEDIUM TURNS
						7 TAKING OFF INTO WIND
						8 POWERED APPROACH AND LANDING
						9 GLIDING APPROACH AND LANDING
	14	MAGISTER	R1848	Sgt JEFFRIES	SELF	15 STEEP TURNS
						16 CLIMBING TURNS
						18. ACTION IN THE EVENT OF FIRE
						18a ABANDONING AN AIRCRAFT

GRAND TOTAL [Cols. (1) to (10)]
.....15.......Hrs....35.........Mins.

TOTALS CARRIED FORWARD

YEAR 1940		AIRCRAFT		PILOT, OR 1ST PILOT	2ND PILOT, PUPIL OR PASSENGER	DUTY (INCLUDING RESULTS AND REMARKS)
MONTH	DATE	Type	No.			
—	—	—	—	—	—	—— TOTALS BROUGHT FORWARD
Oct	15	MAGISTER	R1843	Sgt JEFFRIES	SELF	15 STEEP TURNS 16 CLIMBING TURNS
..	15	MAGISTER	R1843	SELF	—	15 STEEP TURNS 16 CLIMBING TURNS
..	15	MAGISTER	R1843	SELF	—	15 STEEP TURNS 16 CLIMBING TURNS
..	15	MAGISTER	R1840	SELF	—	15 STEEP TURNS 16 CLIMBING TURNS
..	16	MAGISTER	R1966	SELF	—	15 STEEP TURNS 16 CLIMBING TURNS
..	16	MAGISTER	R1901	SELF	—	7 TAKING OFF INTO WIND 8 POWERED APPROACH AND LANDING
..	16	MAGISTER	R1848	Sgt JEFFRIES	SELF	13. PRECAUTIONARY LANDING
..	17	MAGISTER	R1843	SELF	—	13 PRECAUTIONARY LANDING
..	18	MAGISTER	R1901	SELF	—	15. STEEP TURNS 16 CLIMBING TURNS

GRAND TOTAL [Cols. (1) to (10)]
..21.. Hrs. ..15.. Mins.

TOTALS CARRIED FORWARD

YEAR 1940		AIRCRAFT		PILOT, OR 1ST PILOT	2ND PILOT, PUPIL OR PASSENGER	DUTY (INCLUDING RESULTS AND REMARKS)
MONTH	DATE	Type	No.			
—	—	—	—	—	—	—— TOTALS BROUGHT FORWARD
Oct.	18	MAGISTER	R.1843	SELF	—	7 TAKING OFF INTO WIND
						8 POWERED APPROACH AND LANDING
						4 GLIDING APPROACH AND LANDING
,,	18	MAGISTER	R1964	SELF	—	15. STEEP TURNS
						16. CLIMBING TURNS
,,	19	MAGISTER	R1840	Sgt JEFFRIES	SELF	15 STEEP TURNS
						16 CLIMBING TURNS
						21 RESTARTING THE ENGINE IN FLIGHT
,,	19	MAGISTER	R1857	Sgt JEFFRIES	SELF	15 STEEP TURNS
						16 CLIMBING TURNS
,,	19	MAGISTER	R1857	SELF	—	13. PRECAUTIONARY LANDING
,,	19	MAGISTER	R1837	SELF	—	15 STEEP LANDING
						16 CLIMBING TURNS
,,	21	MAGISTER	R3856	SELF	—	15. STEEP TURNS
						16. CLIMBING TURNS

GRAND TOTAL [Cols. (1) to (10)]
25 Hrs 35 Mins.

TOTALS CARRIED FORWARD

YEAR 1940		AIRCRAFT		PILOT, OR 1ST PILOT	2ND PILOT, PUPIL OR PASSENGER	DUTY (INCLUDING RESULTS AND REMARKS)
MONTH	DATE	Type	No.			
		—	—	—	—	— TOTALS BROUGHT FORWARD
Oct.	21	MAGISTER	R1901	SELF	—	6. MEDIUM TURNS
						7. TAKING OFF INTO WIND
						8. POWERED APPROACH AND LANDING
						15. STEEP TURNS
						16. CLIMBING TURNS
"	23	MAGISTER	R1901	F/LT LINES	SELF	13. PRECAUTIONARY LANDING
						14. LOW FLYING
"	24	MAGISTER	L8273	SELF	—	6 MEDIUM TURNS
						7 TAKING OFF INTO WIND
						8 POWERED APPROACH AND LANDING
						15 STEEP TURNS
						16 CLIMBING TURNS
"	24	MAGISTER	R1843	SELF	—	6 MEDIUM TURNS
						13 PRECAUTIONARY LANDING
						15 STEEP TURNS
						16 CLIMBING TURNS
"	24	MAGISTER	R1840	SELF	—	7 TAKING OFF INTO WIND
						8 POWERED APPROACH AND LANDING

GRAND TOTAL [Cols. (1) to (10)]
....29....Hrs....25....Mins.

TOTALS CARRIED FORWARD

~ 174 ~

Year 1940		Aircraft		Pilot, or 1st Pilot	2nd Pilot, Pupil or Passenger	Duty (Including Results and Remarks)
Month	Date	Type	No.			
		—	—	—	—	—— Totals Brought Forward
Oct	25	Magister	R1837	F/Lt Lines	SELF	12 Sideslipping
						17 Forced Landing
"	25	Magister	R.1966	SELF		6 Medium Turns
						12 Sideslipping
						15 Steep Turns
						16 Climbing Turns
"	26	Magister	P2432	SELF	—	6 Medium Turns
						15 Steep Turns
						16 Climbing Turns
"	27	Magister	R.1837	SELF	—	12. Sideslipping
						15. Steep Turns
						16. Climbing Turns
"	27	Magister	P.2432	F/Lt Lines	SELF	19 Instrument Flying
"	28	Magister	R1837	SELF	—	7. Taking off into Wind
						9 Gliding Approach and Landing
						16 Climbing Turns
"	28	Magister	R1837	SELF	—	6. Medium Turns
"	28	Magister	R1966	Sgt Jeffries	SELF	19. Instrument Flying

GRAND TOTAL [Cols. (1) to (10)]
....36....Hrs....35....Mins.

TOTALS CARRIED FORWARD

~ 175 ~

YEAR 1940		AIRCRAFT		PILOT, OR 1ST PILOT	2ND PILOT, PUPIL OR PASSENGER	DUTY (INCLUDING RESULTS AND REMARKS)
MONTH	DATE	Type	No.			
		—	—	—	—	— TOTALS BROUGHT FORWARD
Oct	29	MAGISTER	R.1966	Sgt JEFFRIES	SELF	15. STEEP TURNS
						16 CLIMBING TURNS
						17 FORCED LANDING
						19 INSTRUMENT FLYING
						22. AEROBATICS
..	29	MAGISTER	L8352	SELF	—	7 TAKING OFF INTO WIND
						9 GLIDING APPROACH AND LANDING
						16 CLIMBING TURNS
						22. AEROBATICS
..	29	MAGISTER	R.1966	Sgt JEFFRIES		19. INSTRUMENT FLYING
..	30	MAGISTER	R.1966	Sgt JEFFRIES	SELF	19. INSTRUMENT FLYING
..	31	MAGISTER	R.1966	Sgt JEFFRIES	SELF	23 AIR NAVIGATION
..	31	MAGISTER	R.1966	SELF	—	23 AIR NAVIGATION

GRAND TOTAL [Cols. (1) to (10)]

43 ....Hrs. 00 ....Mins.

TOTALS CARRIED FORWARD

YEAR 1940		AIRCRAFT		PILOT, OR 1ST PILOT	2ND PILOT, PUPIL OR PASSENGER	DUTY (INCLUDING RESULTS AND REMARKS)
MONTH	DATE	Type	No.			
—	—	—	—	—	—	— TOTALS BROUGHT FORWARD
Nov.	1.	MAGISTER	N5409	SELF	—	23. AIR NAVIGATION
"	1	MAGISTER	R1837	SELF	—	22. AEROBATICS 10. SPINNING.
"	2	MAGISTER	R1843	Sgt JEFFRIES	SELF	19. INSTRUMENT FLYING
"	2	MAGISTER	N5404	SELF	—	7 TAKING OFF INTO WIND 9 POWERED APPROACH AND LANDG 15 STEEP TURNS 16 CLIMBING TURNS
"	3	MAGISTER	R1843	Sgt JEFFRIES	SELF	19. INSTRUMENT FLYING 20 TAKING OFF AND LANDING OUT OF WIND
"	3	MAGISTER	N5409	SELF	—	10. SPINNING 15 STEEP TURNS 16 CLIMBING TURNS
"	4	MAGISTER	P2432	SELF	—	17. FORCED LANDING 22. AEROBATICS
"	4	MAGISTER	N9737	F/Lt ADDINSELL	SELF	F/C TEST

GRAND TOTAL [Cols. (1) to (10)] 49 Hrs. 25 Mins.   TOTALS CARRIED FORWARD

YEAR 1940		AIRCRAFT		PILOT, OR 1ST PILOT	2ND PILOT, PUPIL OR PASSENGER	DUTY (INCLUDING RESULTS AND REMARKS)
MONTH	DATE	Type	No.			
		—	—	—	—	—— TOTALS BROUGHT FORWARD
Nov	8	Oxford	6323	Sgt Caen	L.AC. Mason	1. Air Experience
						1A. Familiarity with Cockpit Layout
						2. Effect of Controls
						3 Taxying
						4. Straight and Level Flying
						5. Climbing, Gliding and Stalling
						6 Medium Turns
	9	Oxford	1835	Sgt Caen	Self	6 Medium Turns
						7 Taking off into Wind
						8 Powered Approach and Landing
	10	Oxford	1835	Sgt Caen	Self	6 Medium Turns
						7 Taking off into Wind
						8. Powered Approach and Landing
	11	Oxford	1835	Sgt Caen	Self	6 Medium Turns
						7 Taking off into Wind
						8 Powered Approach and Landing
	13	Oxford	4837	Sgt Caen	Self	6 Medium Turns
						7 Taking off into Wind
						8 Powered Approach and Landing
						9 Action in the event of Fire
						9A Abandoning an Aircraft

GRAND TOTAL [Cols. (1) to (10)]
......52....Hrs....05....Mins.

TOTALS CARRIED FORWARD

YEAR 1940		AIRCRAFT		PILOT, OR 1ST PILOT	2ND PILOT, PUPIL OR: PASSENGER	DUTY (INCLUDING RESULTS AND REMARKS)
MONTH	DATE	Type	No.			
—	—	—	—	—	—	—— TOTALS BROUGHT FORWARD
Nov.	13	Oxford	1193	Sgt. CAEN	SELF	6 MEDIUM TURNS
						7 TAKING OFF INTO WIND
						8 POWERED APPROACH AND LANDING
						9 ACTION IN THE EVENT OF FIRE
						9A ABANDONING AN AIRCRAFT
	14	Oxford	4764	Sgt CAEN	SELF	6 MEDIUM TURNS
						7 TAKING OFF INTO WIND
						9 ACTION IN THE EVENT OF FIRE
	17	Oxford	1193	F/O PULLEN	SELF	7 TAKING OFF INTO WIND
						8 POWERED APPROACH AND LANDING
	18	Oxford	4764	Sgt CAEN	SELF	6 MEDIUM TURNS
						7 TAKING OFF INTO WIND
						8 POWERED APPROACH AND LANDING
	18	Oxford	4764	F/Lt SYMONDSON	SELF	6 MEDIUM TURNS
						7 TAKING OFF INTO WIND
						8 POWERED APPROACH AND LANDING
	21	Oxford	4764	Sgt CAEN	SELF	6 MEDIUM TURNS
						7 TAKING OFF INTO WIND
						8 POWERED APPROACH AND LANDING

GRAND TOTAL [Cols. (1) to (10)]
..56.. Hrs. ..20.. Mins.

TOTALS CARRIED FORWARD

YEAR 1940		AIRCRAFT		PILOT, OR 1ST PILOT	2ND PILOT, PUPIL OR PASSENGER	DUTY (INCLUDING RESULTS AND REMARKS)
MONTH	DATE	Type	No.			
—	—	—	—	—	—	— Totals Brought Forward
Nov	21	Oxford	4764	F/Lt Symondson	SELF	SOLO TEST
	21	Oxford	4764	SELF	—	10. FIRST SOLO
	22	Oxford	1193	Sgt CAEN	SELF	18 NAVIGATION
						14 LOW FLYING
						12 CLIMBING TURNS
						MAP READING
	23	Oxford	1824	Sgt CAEN	SELF	6 MEDIUM TURNS
						7 TAKING OFF INTO WIND
						8 POWERED APPROACH AND LANDING
						11 STEEP TURNS
						12 CLIMBING TURNS
						16 INSTRUMENT FLYING
	25	Oxford	4764	Sgt CAEN	SELF	6 MEDIUM TURNS
						7 TAKING OFF INTO WIND
						8 POWERED APPROACH AND LANDING
	25	Oxford	4764	SELF	—	5 CLIMBING, GLIDING AND STALLING
						6 MEDIUM TURNS
						11 STEEP TURNS
						12 CLIMBING TURNS

GRAND TOTAL [Cols. (1) to (10)]
......61....Hrs...00...........Mins.

TOTALS CARRIED FORWARD

First solo flight in an Oxford on 21st November.

YEAR 1940		AIRCRAFT		PILOT, OR 1st PILOT	2ND PILOT, PUPIL OR PASSENGER	DUTY (INCLUDING RESULTS AND REMARKS)
MONTH	DATE	Type	No.			
—	—	—	—	—	—	— TOTALS BROUGHT FORWARD
Nov	26	Oxford	1834	SELF	—	6 MEDIUM TURNS
						7 TAKING OFF INTO WIND
						8 POWERED APPROACH AND LANDING
						11 STEEP TURNS
						12 CLIMBING TURNS
	27	Oxford	6805	Sgt CAEN	SELF	6 MEDIUM TURNS
						7 TAKING OFF INTO WIND
						8 POWERED APPROACH AND LANDING
						13 GLIDING APPROACH AND LANDING
	28	Oxford	4764	Sgt CAEN	SELF	INSTRUMENT FLYING
						NAVIGATION
	28	Oxford	4764	SELF	—	MAP READING
	29	Oxford	1824	SELF	—	7 TAKING OFF INTO WIND
						13. GLIDING APPROACH AND LANDING

No. 1A FLYING
SCHOOL R.A.F.

CHIEF FLYING
DATE 5/12/40 INSTRUCTOR.

Summary for NOVEMBER 1940
Unit No 1A S.F.T.S.
Date 3.12.40
Signature ....

Aircraft Types.
1. OXFORD
2. ....
3. ....
4. ....

GRAND TOTAL [Cols. (1) to (10)]
57 Hrs. 00 Mins.

TOTALS CARRIED FORWARD

~ 181 ~

YEAR 1940		AIRCRAFT		PILOT, OR 1ST PILOT	2ND PILOT, PUPIL OR PASSENGER	DUTY (INCLUDING RESULTS AND REMARKS)
MONTH	DATE	Type	No.			
		—	—	—	—	TOTALS BROUGHT FORWARD
DEC.	2	OXFORD	1824	Sgt. CAEN	SELF	15B. PRECAUTIONARY LANDING. FULL POWER
''	2	OXFORD	1824	SELF	—	15B PRECAUTIONARY LANDING. FULL POWER
''	3	OXFORD	1193	Sgt. CAEN	SELF	15B PRECAUTIONARY LANDING. FULL POWER CRASHED
''	18	OXFORD	6370	Sgt. CAEN	SELF	16. INSTRUMENT FLYING
''	22	OXFORD	4799	SELF	—	15B. PRECAUTIONARY LANDING. FULL POWER 6 MEDIUM TURNS 7 TAKING OFF INTO WIND 9 POWERED APPROACH AND LANDING
''	23	OXFORD	6550	SELF	—	5 CLIMBING GLIDING AND STALLING 6 MEDIUM TURNS 7 TAKING OFF INTO WIND 8 POWERED APPROACH AND LANDING
''	24	OXFORD	6370	Sgt CAEN	SELF	15A. PRECAUTIONARY LANDING. HALF POWER
''	24	OXFORD	6370	SELF	—	15A. PRECAUTIONARY LANDING. HALF POWER
''	28	OXFORD	1824	Sgt CAEN	SELF	16. INSTRUMENT FLYING
				GRAND TOTAL [Cols. (1) to (10)] .....7.4.....Hrs.....1.0.....Mins.		TOTALS CARRIED FORWARD

Crashed on December 3rd (see page 13).

YEAR 1941		AIRCRAFT		PILOT, OR 1ST PILOT	2ND PILOT, PUPIL OR PASSENGER	DUTY (INCLUDING RESULTS AND REMARKS
MONTH	DATE	Type	No.			
		—	—	—	—	TOTALS BROUGHT FORWARD
JAN	2	OXFORD	6805	W/O BROWN	SELF	NAVIGATION TEST
"	3	OXFORD	6323	SELF		11. STEEP TURNS
						15A PRECAUTIONARY LANDINGS, HALF P...
						15B PRECAUTIONARY LANDINGS FULL POW...
"	3	OXFORD	6323	SELF		No. 1. X COUNTRY CRANFIE...
						-WORCESTER-CRANFIELD (ABANDONED
"	3	OXFORD	6323	SELF		11. STEEP TURNS
						12. CLIMBING TURNS
						13. GLIDING APPROACH AND LANDIN...
"	4	OXFORD	6370	SELF		No. 1. X COUNTRY CRANFIE...
						WORCESTER-SHAWBURY-WORCESTER-CRANFI...
"	4	OXFORD	8980	Sgt. CAEN	SELF	A/C. TEST
"	4	OXFORD	8980	Sgt. CAEN	SELF	6 MEDIUM TURNS
						7 TAKING OFF INTO WIND
						8 POWERED APPROACH AND LANDI...
						9. ACTION IN THE EVENT OF FIR...
"	4	OXFORD	8980	SELF		6 MEDIUM TURNS
						7 TAKING OFF INTO WIND
						8. POWERED APPROACH AND LANDI...

GRAND TOTAL [Cols. (1) to (10)]

83 Hrs. 20 Mins.

TOTALS CARRIED FOR...

YEAR 1941		AIRCRAFT		PILOT, OR 1ST PILOT	2ND PILOT, PUPIL OR PASSENGER	DUTY (INCLUDING RESULTS AND REMARKS)
MONTH	DATE	Type	No.			
		—	—	—	—	—— TOTALS BROUGHT FORWARD
JAN	4	OXFORD	6805	F/O PULLEN	SELF	7. TAKING OFF INTO WIND
						8. POWERED APPROACH AND LAND
"	9	OXFORD	6370	Sgt CAEN	SELF.	16. INSTRUMENT FLYING
						RECOVERIES
"	9	OXFORD	4630	SELF	LAC. NASH	16. INSTRUMENT FLYING
"	9	OXFORD	4630	LAC NASH	SELF	16 INSTRUMENT FLYING
"	12	OXFORD	6370	SELF	—	REVISION
"	12	OXFORD	6370	SELF	LAC. GLOCK	16. INSTRUMENT FLYING
"	12	OXFORD	6370	LAC. GLOCK	SELF	16 INSTRUMENT FLYING
"	13	OXFORD	6370	Sgt CAEN	SELF	7. TAKING OFF INTO WINDS
						8. POWERED APPROACH AND LANDI
"	13	OXFORD	6370	Sgt CAEN	SELF	7 TAKING OFF INTO WIND
						8. POWERED APPROACH AND LAND

GRAND TOTAL [Cols. (1) to (10)]

84 Hrs. 55 Mins.

TOTALS CARRIED FORW

YEAR 1941		AIRCRAFT		PILOT, OR 1ST PILOT	2ND PILOT, PUPIL OR PASSENGER	DUTY (INCLUDING RESULTS AND REMARKS
MONTH	DATE	Type	No.			
—	—	—	—	—	—	— TOTALS BROUGHT FORWARD
JAN	14	OXFORD	1835	SELF	LAC. MASON	11. STEEP TURNS
						13. GLIDING APPROACH AND LANDING
						16. INSTRUMENT FLYING
''	14	OXFORD	1835	LAC. MASON	SELF	11. STEEP TURNS
						12. CLIMBING TURNS
''	15	OXFORD	1835	SELF	—	11 STEEP TURNS
						13. GLIDING APPROACH AND LANDING
						15A. PRECAUTIONARY LANDING
''	16	OXFORD	4655	LAC. MASON	SELF	W/S AND D.
''	16	OXFORD	4655	SELF	LAC. MASON	W/S AND D
''	17	OXFORD	3641	SELF	—	7 TAKING OFF INTO WIND
						8. POWERED APPROACH AND LAND
''	19	OXFORD	4638	SGT KILNER	LAC. LOWMAN	7 TAKING OFF INTO WIND
						8. POWERED APPROACH AND LAND
''	19	OXFORD	4630	SGT KILNER	SELF	7. TAKING OFF INTO WIND
						8. POWERED APPROACH AND LANDING

GRAND TOTAL [Cols. (1) to (10)]
90 Hrs. 30 Mins.

TOTALS CARRIED FOR

YEAR 1941		AIRCRAFT		PILOT, OR 1ST PILOT	2ND PILOT, PUPIL OR PASSENGER	DUTY (INCLUDING RESULTS AND REMARKS)
MONTH	DATE	Type	No.			
—	—	—	—	—	—	—— TOTALS BROUGHT FORWARD
FEB.	1.	OXFORD	6805	Sgt CAEN	SELF	11. STEEP TURNS
						13. GLIDING APPROACH AND LANDING
						16. INSTRUMENT FLYING
"	1	OXFORD	6805	SELF	—	11. STEEP TURNS
						13. GLIDING APPROACH AND LANDING
"	2	OXFORD	3676	LAC LEE	SELF	No. 2. I.F. CROSS-COUNTRY
						CRANFIELD · MKT HARBOROUGH ·
						C. NORTON - CRANFIELD
"	2	OXFORD	3676	SELF	—	7. TAKING OFF INTO WIND
						8. POWERED APPROACH AND LANDING
						13. GLIDING APPROACH AND LANDING
"	3	OXFORD	6550	Sgt CAEN	SELF	7. TAKING OFF INTO WIND
						8. POWERED APPROACH AND LANDING
"	3	OXFORD	6550	Sgt CAEN	SELF	7 TAKING OFF INTO WIND
						8. POWERED APPROACH AND LANDING
"	4	OXFORD	6550	SELF	LAC MASON	No. 2. CROSS-COUNTRY.
						CRANFIELD · BATH · READING
						PRECAUTIONARY LANDING AT
						KINGS LANGLEY

GRAND TOTAL [Cols. (1) to (10)] ....97....Hrs....25....Mins. TOTALS CARRIED FORWARD

Precautionary landing on Feb 4th which led to attending a Dorchester 'do' (see page 21)

YEAR 1941		AIRCRAFT		PILOT, OR 1ST PILOT	2ND PILOT, PUPIL OR PASSENGER	DUTY (INCLUDING RESULTS AND REMARKS)
MONTH	DATE	Type	No.			
—	—	—	—	—	—	— TOTALS BROUGHT FORWARD
FEB.	7	OXFORD	3672	SELF	—	11. STEEP TURNS
						13. GLIDING APPROACH AND LANDING
						15A. PRECAUTIONARY LANDING (HALF FLAP)
..	8	OXFORD	6375	SELF	—	7 TAKING OFF INTO WIND
						8. POWERED APPROACH AND LANDING
						11. STEEP TURNS
..	8	OXFORD	4630	SELF	LAC. FORREST	No. 2. CROSS-COUNTRY
						CRANFIELD - BATH - READING -
						WOLVERTON - CRANFIELD
..	9	OXFORD	1968	SELF	—	15B PRECAUTIONARY LANDINGS
..	9	OXFORD	3676	Sgt. CAEN	SELF	17 NIGHT FLYING
						1. LANDING.
..	10	OXFORD	8968	LAC. MASON	SELF	No. 2. CROSS-COUNTRY
						CRANFIELD - BATH - READING
						WOLVERTON - CRANFIELD
..	11	OXFORD	4572	LAC FOSTER	SELF	CAMERA OBSCURA
..	11	OXFORD	6333	SELF	LAC FOSTER	CAMERA OBSCURA

GRAND TOTAL [Cols. (1) to (10)]

103 Hrs. 55 Mins.

TOTALS CARRIED FORWARD

YEAR 1941		AIRCRAFT		PILOT, OR 1ST PILOT	2ND PILOT, PUPIL OR PASSENGER	DUTY (INCLUDING RESULTS AND REMARKS)
MONTH	DATE	Type	No.			
—	—	—	—	—	—	— TOTALS BROUGHT FORWARD
FEB.	12	OXFORD	1954	SELF	—	7. TAKING OFF INTO WIND
						8. POWERED APPROACH AND LAND
··	14	OXFORD	6805	SELF	LAC. FOSTER	No. 2. I.F. CROSS-COUNTRY
						CRANFIELD - MKE. HARBOROUGH
						C. NORTON. CRANFIELD
··	15	OXFORD	8968	LAC FOSTER	SELF	No. 3. CROSS-COUNTRY
						CRANFIELD - FINNINGLEY
						PETERBORO' RATCLIFFE - CRANF
··	15	OXFORD	6805	Sgt CAEN	SELF	FORMATION. 1. 2. 3. PASS
··	15	OXFORD	3641	Sgt CAEN	SELF	FORMATION 1.
						11. STEEP TURNS
						15A PRECAUTIONARY LANDING PO
··	15	OXFORD	3641	F/O PULLEN	SELF	17. NIGHT FLYING. 4 LANDIN
··	15	OXFORD	3641	SELF	—	17. NIGHT FLYING. 1. LANDING
FEB	17	OXFORD	6805	SELF	Sgt JOHNSON	16. INSTRUMENT FLYING
						11. STEEP TURNS

GRAND TOTAL [Cols. (1) to (10)]
.................Hrs.................Mins.

TOTALS CARRIED FOR

~ 188 ~

YEAR 1941		AIRCRAFT		PILOT, OR 1ST PILOT	2ND PILOT, PUPIL OR PASSENGER	DUTY (INCLUDING RESULTS AND REMARKS)
MONTH	DATE	Type	No.			
—	—	—	—	—	—	——— TOTALS BROUGHT FORWARD
APRIL	11	OXFORD	6551	F/LT FARTHING	SELF	6. MEDIUM TURNS
						7. TAKING OFF INTO WIND
						8. POWERED APPROACH AND LANDIN
						11. STEEP TURNS.
						16. INSTRUMENT FLYING
"	12	OXFORD	6551	SELF		7. TAKING OFF INTO WIND
						8. POWERED APPROACH AND LAN
						11. STEEP TURNS
"	12	OXFORD	9656	SELF		11. STEEP TURNS
						15B. PRECAUTIONARY LANDINGS
						FULL POWER
"	13	OXFORD	4587	F/O MAYCOCK	SELF	R/T. AIR TO AIR
						AIR TO GROUND
"	13	OXFORD	6551	SELF	CPL. PARK	No. 3 CROSS-COUNTRY
						CRANFIELD. FINNINGLEY. PETERB
						RATCLIFFE. CRANFIELD
"	14	OXFORD	6551	SELF		7. TAKING OFF INTO WIND
						8. POWERED APPROACH AND LAN

GRAND TOTAL [Cols. (1) to (10)]
.....115.....Hrs...50.........Mins.

TOTALS CARRIED FORWA

Year 1941		Aircraft		Pilot, or 1st Pilot	2nd Pilot, Pupil or Passenger	Duty (Including Results and Remarks)
Month	Date	Type	No.			
—	—	—	—	—	—	—— Totals Brought Forward
April	15.	Oxford	4581.	L.AC. Taylor	SELF	Pass Navigator. No.4. X. Country CRANFIELD. Moreton in Marsh. Halton Swindon. Wolverton. Cranfield
"	15	Oxford	4581	SELF	LAC. Taylor	No.4 X. Country. Cranfield. Moreton in Marsh. Halton Swindon. Wolverton. Cranfield
"	15	Oxford	4582	Cpl Ward	SELF	Passenger Instrument Flying
"	15	Oxford	4582	SELF	Cpl Ward	16. Instrument Flying
"	17	Oxford	6345	SELF	LAC. Taylor	No.5. X. Country. Cranfield Oakham. Reading. Ashchurch. Bourne. Cranfield
"	17	Oxford	6345	SELF	LAC. Dale	Cranfield. - Sibson
"	17	Oxford	5945	F/o White	SELF	17. Night Flying 2. Landings
"	17	Oxford	5945	F/o White	SELF	17. Night Flying L. Landing

GRAND TOTAL [Cols. (1) to (10)]
.....122....Hrs....30.........Mins.

Totals Carried Forward

~ 190 ~

YEAR 1941		AIRCRAFT		PILOT, OR 1ST PILOT	2ND PILOT, PUPIL OR PASSENGER	DUTY (INCLUDING RESULTS AND REMARKS)
MONTH	DATE	Type	No.			
—	—	—	—	—	—	—— TOTALS BROUGHT FORWARD
APRIL	17	OXFORD	5945	SELF	—	12. NIGHT FLYING. 6. LANDINGS
..	18	OXFORD	9024	SELF	—	7 TAKING OFF INTO WIND 8. POWERED APPROACH AND LANDING
..	20	OXFORD	4582	SELF	—	11. STEEP TURNS 13. GLIDING APPROACH AND LANDING
..	20	OXFORD	9656	LAC. DALE	SELF	PASS NAVIGATOR. CRANFIELD OAKHAM READING ASHCHURCH BOURNE CRANFIELD
..	21	OXFORD	4587	P/o ATTWATER	SELF	7 TAKING OFF INTO WIND 8 POWERED APPROACH AND LANDING 13. GLIDING APPROACH AND LANDING SINGLE-ENGINED FLYING
..	21	OXFORD	4739	P/o CLARKE	SELF	CRANFIELD-SIBSON. PASSENGER
..	24	OXFORD	4834	F/o WHITE	SELF	FLIGHT COMMANDER'S TEST
..	24	OXFORD	4834	SELF	—	15A PRECAUTIONARY LANDING HALF POWER 15B PRECAUTIONARY LANDING FULL POWER

GRAND TOTAL [Cols. (1) to (10)]
128 Hrs. 30 Mins.

TOTALS CARRIED FORWARD

~ 191 ~

YEAR 1941		AIRCRAFT		PILOT, OR 1ST PILOT	2ND PILOT, PUPIL OR PASSENGER	DUTY (INCLUDING RESULTS AND REMARKS)
MONTH	DATE	Type	No.			
—	—	—	—	—	—	—— TOTALS BROUGHT FORWARD
APRIL	24	OXFORD	5945	F/O MAYCOCK	SELF	17. NIGHT FLYING
						2. LANDINGS
"	24	OXFORD	5945	SELF	—	17. NIGHT FLYING
						2. LANDINGS
"	26	OXFORD	9024	SELF	—	11. STEEP TURNS
						15A PRECAUTIONARY LANDING
						HALF POWER
						15B. PRECAUTIONARY LANDINGS
						FULL POWER
"	26	OXFORD	9656	SELF	LAC GILMOUR	16. INSTRUMENT FLYING
"	26	OXFORD	9656	LAC GILMOUR	SELF	16 INSTRUMENT FLYING. PASSENGER
"	27	OXFORD	4834	P/O ATTWATER	SELF	PASSENGER. Z. Z.
"	27	OXFORD	4834	P/O ATTWATER	SELF	Z. Z. APPROACH
"	28	OXFORD	3673	F/LT BURGE	SELF	C.F.I's "END OF TERM TEST"
"	28	OXFORD	4639	SELF	—	11. STEEP TURNS
						13 GLIDING APPROACH AND LANDING

GRAND TOTAL [Cols. (1) to (10)]   TOTALS CARRIED FORWARD

132 Hrs. 45 Mins.

| YEAR 1941 | | AIRCRAFT | | PILOT, OR | 2ND PILOT, PUPIL | DUTY |
MONTH	DATE	Type	No.	1ST PILOT	OR PASSENGER	(INCLUDING RESULTS AND REMARKS)
—	—	—	—	—	—	— TOTALS BROUGHT FORWARD
APRIL	29	OXFORD	4639	SELF	→	FORMATION. 1. 2. 3.
				SUMMARY FOR FEBRUARY AND APRIL		OXFORD
				UNIT 14. S. FTS		
				DATE 1·5·41		AIRCRAFT TYPES
				SIGNATURE *Haycock* F/L.		
MAY	1	OXFORD	4557	SELF	→	FORMATION. 1. 2. 3.
				SUMMARY FOR MAY		OXFORD
				UNIT 14. S. F. TS.		
				DATE 6·5·41		AIRCRAFT TYPES
				SIGNATURE *Haycock* F/L.		

GRAND TOTAL [Cols. (1) to (10)]
135 Hrs. 45 Mins.

TOTALS CARRIED FORWARD

SINGLE-ENGINE AIRCRAFT				MULTI-ENGINE AIRCRAFT						PASS-ENGER	INSTR./CLOUD FLYING [Incl. in cols. (1) to (10)]	
DAY		NIGHT		DAY			NIGHT					
DUAL	PILOT	DUAL	PILOT	DUAL	1ST PILOT	2ND PILOT	DUAL	1ST PILOT	2ND PILOT		DUAL	PILOT
(1)	(2)	(3)	(4)	(5)	(6)	(7)	(8)	(9)	(10)	(11)	(12)	(13)
24.50	25.45			28.45	52.00		2.45	1.40		22.40	10.40	5.00

PROFICIENCY AS PILOT ON TYPE — *Above Average*

to be assessed :- EXCEPTIONAL; ABOVE THE AVERAGE; AVERAGE; BELOW THE AVERAGE.

any ... faults in flying which must be watched :

E.R. Shepard W/Cdr
Flying Wing 148 F.T.S.   Officer Commanding ...... ROYAL AIR FORCE
7/3/41.

Year 1941		Aircraft		Pilot, or 1st Pilot	2nd Pilot, Pupil or Passenger	Duty (Including Results and Remarks)
Month	Date	Type	No.			
—	—	—	—	—	—	— Totals Brought Forward
		Certified that I fully understand the Petrol, Oil, and Ignition Systems of the Blenheim Aircraft, the Hydraulic system, and the correct sequence of operation controls. Sgd. G. L. Shackleton.				
June	14	Blenheim	1343	F/Lt. Nicol	Self	5 Landings
"	14	Blenheim	7115	F/Lt Nicol	Self	4 Landings
	16	Blenheim	7115	F/Lt Nicol	Self	3 Landings
"	16	Blenheim	7115	Self	— — 1	3 Landings
"	16	Blenheim	7115	F/Lt Nicol	Self	3 Landings and I.F.
"	16	Blenheim	7115	Self	— —	3 Landings
"	18	Blenheim	6800	Self	—	6 Landings
"	18	Blenheim	1250	F/Lt Nicol	Self	Instrument Flying
"	19	Blenheim	6800	Self	—	4 Landings
				Grand Total [Cols. (1) to (10)] .....146.....Hrs.....20.....Mins.		Totals Carried Forward

Gordon moves from Oxfords to Blenheims.

Year 1941		Aircraft		Pilot, or 1st Pilot	2nd Pilot, Pupil or Passenger	Duty (Including Results and Remarks)
Month	Date	Type	No.			
—	—	—	—	—	—	Totals Brought Forward
June	20	BLENHEIM	1140	F/Lt Nicol	SELF	INSTRUMENT FLYING
"	20	BLENHEIM	4838	SELF	—	4 LANDINGS
"	23	BLENHEIM	4871	SELF	Sgt EYRES	LOW LEVEL BOMBING
"	23	BLENHEIM	4891	SELF	Sgt EYRES	LOW LEVEL BOMBING
"	24	BLENHEIM	3626	SELF	Sgt EYRES	LOW LEVEL BOMBING
"	24	BLENHEIM	3626	SELF	Sgt EYRES	HIGH LEVEL BOMBING
"	27	BLENHEIM	5566	SELF	Sgt EYRES	SHALLOW DIVE BOMBING
"	29	BLENHEIM	3626	SELF	Sgt EYRES	HIGH LEVEL BOMBING
"	29	BLENHEIM	3626	SELF	Sgt EYRES	LOW LEVEL BOMBING
"	29	BLENHEIM	4865	SELF	Sgt EYRES	SHALLOW DIVE BOMBING
			GRAND TOTAL [Cols. (1) to (10)] 153 Hrs. 05 Mins.			Totals Carried Forward

~ 196 ~

YEAR 1941		AIRCRAFT		PILOT, OR 1ST PILOT	2ND PILOT, PUPIL OR PASSENGER	DUTY (INCLUDING RESULTS AND REMARKS)
MONTH	DATE	Type	No.			
—	—	—	—	—	—	—— TOTALS BROUGHT FORWARD
JULY	1.	BLENHEIM	3625	SELF	Sgt EYRES	LOW LEVEL BOMBING
''	3	BLENHEIM	4871	SELF	Sgt EYRES	HIGH LEVEL BOMBING
''	3	BLENHEIM	5566	SELF	Sgt EYRES	HIGH LEVEL BOMBING
''	7	BLENHEIM	5566	SELF	Sgt EYRES	HIGH LEVEL BOMBING
''	19	BLENHEIM	9412	SELF	Sgt EYRES Sgt KENNEDY	BASE - CHURCH FENTON - MELTON MOWBRAY - BASE
''	20	BLENHEIM	6166	SELF	Sgt EYRES Sgt KENNEDY	BASE - STOW IN WOLD - HULLAVINGTON - BASE
''	30	BLENHEIM	2781	SELF	Sgt EYRES Sgt KENNEDY	BASE - WORCESTER - SHREWSBURY - MELTON MOWBRAY - TOWCESTER - BASE
''	31	BLENHEIM	6166	SELF	Sgt EYRES Sgt KENNEDY	BASE - BRIZE NORTON - SHREWSBURY GAINSBORO' - BOURNE - BASE

Summary for JUNE & JULY 1941
Unit 17. O.T.U.   Aircraft
Date 1st August   Types
Signature C. Shackleton

1. BLENHEIM
2. _____
3. _____
4. _____

GRAND TOTAL [Cols. (1) to (10)]
................Hrs...................Mins.

TOTALS CARRIED FORWARD

~ 197 ~

YEAR 1941		AIRCRAFT		PILOT, OR 1ST PILOT	2ND PILOT, PUPIL OR PASSENGER	DUTY (INCLUDING RESULTS AND REMARKS)
MONTH	DATE	Type	No.			
—	—	—	—	—	—	TOTALS BROUGHT FORWARD
Aug.	5	BLENHEIM	5885	SELF	Sgt EYRES Sgt KENNEDY	FORMATION - BASE - LITTLE RISLINGTON - SHREWSBURY -HAMSWELL - BASE
	6	BLENHEIM	5885	SELF	Sgt EYRES	ZZ AT WYTON. N.C.O. SHALLOW DIVE BOMBING
	6	BLENHEIM	1245	Sgt WILLIAMS	SELF	4 NIGHT LANDINGS
	6	BLENHEIM	6959	SELF	Sgt KENNEDY	3 NIGHT LANDINGS
	7	BLENHEIM	6324	SELF	Sgt EYRES Sgt KENNEDY	ZZ AT WYTON D.C.O.
	9	BLENHEIM	5947	SELF	Sgt BAXTER Sgt EYRES Sgt ARCHER	FORMATION, BASE - LITTLE RISLINGTON - SHREWSBURY. HAMSWELL - BASE
	11	BLENHEIM	5899	SELF	Sgt EYRES Sgt KENNEDY	BASE - DISHFORTH - POSN 54°11' 01.00'E - POSN 54° 25'N. 01.40' - POSN 53° 20'N. 01°40'E - SCAMPTON - SPALDING - HOLBECH - BASE
	12	BLENHEIM	5947	SELF	Sgt EYRES Sgt KENNEDY	LOCAL FORMATION

GRAND TOTAL [Cols. (1) to (10)]
....179....Hrs....15......Mins.

TOTALS CARRIED FORWARD

~ 198 ~

(3332—117) Wt. 25808—1966 35,000 8/39 T.S 700

FORM 414 (A)

SUMMARY of FLYING and ASSESSMENTS FOR ~~YEAR~~ *PERIOD* COMMENCING 1st **JUNE - 14th AUGUST** *19.41*

* For Officer, Insert "JUNE"; For Airman Pilot, Insert "AUGUST."]

	S.E. AIRCRAFT		M.E. AIRCRAFT		TOTAL for year PERIOD	GRAND TOTAL All Service Flying
	Day	Night	Day	Night		
DUAL	—	—	6.35	1.45	8.20	64.40
PILOT	—	—	35.10	.50	36.00	115.25
PASSENGER	—	—	—	—		

ASSESSMENT of ABILITY

(To be assessed as :—Exceptional, Above the Average, Average, or Below the Average)

(i) AS A M.E. † PILOT .... *Above the Average*

(ii) AS PILOT–NAVIGATOR/NAVIGATOR ....

(iii) IN BOMBING ....

(iv) IN AIR GUNNERY ....

† Insert :—"P.", "L.B.", "G.R.", "F.B.", etc.

ANY POINTS IN FLYING OR AIRMANSHIP WHICH SHOULD BE WATCHED.

....

....

Signature .... W/Cdr

Date .. 22.8.41 ....

Officer Commanding .. O.C. TRAINING WING, No. 17 O.T.U.

~ 199 ~

YEAR 1941		AIRCRAFT		PILOT, OR 1ST PILOT	2ND PILOT, PUPIL OR PASSENGER	DUTY (INCLUDING RESULTS AND REMARKS)
MONTH	DATE	Type	No.			
—	—	—	—	—	Sgt EYRES Sgt KENNEDY	TOTALS BROUGHT FORWARD
AUG	25	BLENHEIM	2224	SELF	Sgt EYRES Sgt KENNEDY	LOCAL FORMATION
"	25	BLENHEIM	2224	SELF	Sgt EYRES Sgt KENNEDY	LOCAL FORMATION
"	27	BLENHEIM	2224	SELF	Sgt EYRES Sgt KENNEDY	LOW LEVEL PRACTICE BOMBING
"	28	BLENHEIM	2224	SELF	Sgt EYRES Sgt KENNEDY	ARMY Co-op Ex
"	28	BLENHEIM	2224	SELF	Sgt EYRES Sgt KENNEDY	ARMY Co-op Ex
"	28	BLENHEIM	8800	SELF	Sgt EYRES Sgt KENNEDY	ARMY Co-op Ex
"	28	BLENHEIM	8800	SELF	Sgt EYRES Sgt KENNEDY	ARMY Co-op Ex
"	29	BLENHEIM	8800	SELF	Sgt EYRES Sgt KENNEDY	ARMY Co-op Ex
"	29	BLENHEIM	8800	SELF	Sgt EYRES Sgt KENNEDY	ARMY Co-op Ex
"	29	BLENHEIM	5726	SELF	Sgt EYRES Sgt KENNEDY	ARMY Co-op Ex
"	29	BLENHEIM	5726	SELF	Sgt EYRES Sgt KENNEDY	ARMY Co-op Ex

GRAND TOTAL [Cols. (1) to (10)]
189 Hrs. 55 Mins.

TOTALS CARRIED FORWARD

| YEAR | | AIRCRAFT | | PILOT, OR | 2ND PILOT, PUPIL | DUTY |
MONTH	DATE	Type	No.	1ST PILOT	OR PASSENGER	(INCLUDING RESULTS AND REMARKS)
—	—	—	—	—	—	— Totals Brought Forward
AUG	31	BLENHEIM	7307	SELF	Sgt EYRES Sgt KENNEDY	OPERATION TO LILLE CIRCUS AT 14000 ft.
				SUMMARY for AUGUST 1941		BLENHEIM
				UNIT 114 SQDN. AIRCRAFT		
				DATE 1.9.41. TYPES		
				SIGNATURE		
				[signature] S.L.D.		
				O.C. A FLT		
				114 SQDN		

GRAND TOTAL [Cols. (1) to (10)]
192 Hrs. 30 Mins.

TOTALS CARRIED FORWARD

A circis to Lille (see page 30)

YEAR 941		AIRCRAFT		PILOT, OR	2ND PILOT, PUPIL	DUTY
MONTH	DATE	Type	No.	1ST PILOT	OR PASSENGER	(INCLUDING RESULTS AND REMARKS)
—	—	—	—	—	Sgt EYRES Sgt KENNEDY	—— TOTALS BROUGHT FORWARD
EP.	1	BLENHEIM	7307	SELF	Sgt EYRES Sgt KENNEDY	OPERATION RECALLED
	2	BLENHEIM	7307	SELF	Sgt EYRES Sgt KENNEDY	LOW LEVEL PRACTICE BOMBING
	3	BLENHEIM	7307	SELF	Sgt EYRES Sgt KENNEDY	LOCAL FORMATION
	4	BLENHEIM	7307	SELF	Sgt EYRES Sgt KENNEDY	CIRCUS to CHERBOURG 8000 INTENSE HEAVY AND LIGHT FLAK
	6	BLENHEIM	7307	SELF	Sgt EYRES Sgt KENNEDY	LOW LEVEL PRACTICE BOMBING
	7	BLENHEIM	7307	SELF	Sgt EYRES Sgt KENNEDY	BASE - BODNEY - BASE - HORSHAM
	8	BLENHEIM	7307	SELF	Sgt EYRES Sgt KENNEDY	HORSHAM - BASE
	10	BLENHEIM	7307	SELF	Sgt EYRES Sgt KENNEDY	SHIPPING BEAT RECALLED
	11	BLENHEIM	7307	SELF	Sgt EYRES Sgt KENNEDY	SHIPPING BEAT off DUTCH COAST. NOTHING SIGHTED
	15	BLENHEIM	7307	SELF	Sgt EYRES Sgt KENNEDY	BEAT 7. FRISIAN ISLES. CONVOY ATTACKED.

GRAND TOTAL [Cols. (1) to (10)]
206 Hrs. 25 Mins.

TOTALS CARRIED FORWARD   24

YEAR 1941		AIRCRAFT		PILOT, OR 1ST PILOT	2ND PILOT, PUPIL OR PASSENGER	DUTY (INCLUDING RESULTS AND REMARKS)
MONTH	DATE	Type	No.			
—	—	—	—	—	—	— TOTALS BROUGHT FORWARD
SEP.	16	BLENHEIM	7307	SELF	Sgt EYRES Sgt KENNEDY	AIR FIRING AND LOW LEVEL
	17	BLENHEIM	7307	SELF	Sgt EYRES Sgt KENNEDY	CIRCUS TO MAZINGARBE 12000 SLIGHT FLAK
	18	BLENHEIM	7307	SELF		AIR TEST
	20	BLENHEIM	7307	SELF	Sgt EYRES Sgt KENNEDY	BASE - IBSLEY
	20	BLENHEIM	7307	SELF	Sgt EYRES Sgt KENNEDY	CIRCUS TO CHERBOURG 1200 SLIGHT FLAK
	22	BLENHEIM	7307	SELF	Sgt EYRES Sgt KENNEDY	LOCAL FORMATION
	22	BLENHEIM	7307	SELF	Sgt EYRES Sgt KENNEDY	LOW LEVEL PRACTICE BOMBING
	24	BLENHEIM	7302	SELF	Sgt EYRES Sgt KENNEDY	HIGH LEVEL PRACTICE BOMBING
	27	BLENHEIM	7307	SELF	Sgt EYRES Sgt KENNEDY	CIRCUS TO MAZINGARBE 14000' SLIGHT FLAK
	28	BLENHEIM	7307	SELF	Sgt EYRES Sgt KENNEDY Ac. PURKISS	BASE-MOLESWORTH-BASE

GRAND TOTAL [Cols. (1) to (10)]
220 Hrs. 30 Mins.

TOTALS CARRIED FORWARD

YEAR 1941		AIRCRAFT		PILOT, OR 1ST PILOT	2ND PILOT, PUPIL OR PASSENGER	DUTY (INCLUDING RESULTS AND REMARKS)
MONTH	DATE	Type	No.			
—	—	—	—	—	—	— TOTALS BROUGHT FORWARD
		J.Thewbury S/LDR				W/C
		O.C "A" FLIGHT				O.C. 114. SQDN.
Oct.	1	BLENHEIM	7307	SELF	Sgt EYRES Sgt KENNEDY	ARMY Co-op EXERCISES
"	1	BLENHEIM	7307	SELF	Sgt EYRES Sgt KENNEDY	ARMY Co-op EXERCISES
"	2	BLENHEIM	7307	SELF	Sgt EYRES Sgt KENNEDY	ARMY Co-op EXERCISES
"	2	BLENHEIM	7307	SELF	Sgt EYRES Sgt KENNEDY	ARMY Co-op EXERCISES
"	2	BLENHEIM	7307	SELF	Sgt EYRES Sgt KENNEDY	ARMY Co-op EXERCISES
"	13	BLENHEIM	7307	SELF	Sgt EYRES Sgt KENNEDY	CIRCUS AT 14000 Ft TO MAZINGARBE. CONTINUOUS HEAVY FLAK FROM MARDYKE
"	14	BLENHEIM	7307	SELF	Sgt EYRES Sgt KENNEDY	LOCAL FORMATION
				GRAND TOTAL [Cols. (1) to (10)] 229 Hrs. 20 Mins.		TOTALS CARRIED FORWARD

YEAR		AIRCRAFT		PILOT, OR	2ND PILOT, PUPIL	DUTY
MONTH	DATE	Type	No.	1ST PILOT	OR PASSENGER	(INCLUDING RESULTS AND REMARKS)
—	—	—	—	—		— Totals Brought Forward
OCT.	15	BLENHEIM	7307	SELF	Sgt EYRES Sgt KENNEDY	SHIPPING 13 EAT. N° 8. LARGE CONVOY SIGHTED AND ATTACKED. 1 SUNK. SLIGHT FLAK OPPOSITION
	20	BLENHEIM	7307	SELF	Sgt EYRES Sgt KENNEDY	FIGHTER AFFILIATION
	23	BLENHEIM	7307	SELF	Sgt EYRES Sgt KENNEDY	BASE - RED ROUTH
	23	BLENHEIM	7307	SELF	Sgt EYRES Sgt KENNEDY	CIRCUS AT 10000 Ft FROM RED ROUTH TO LANNION. NO FLAK. RUNAWAY HIT

[signature] /LDR.
O.C. "A" FLIGHT

[signature] W/C
O.C. 114 SQUADRON

						GRAND TOTAL [Cols. (1) to (10)]
						240 Hrs. 20 Mins.

TOTALS CARRIED FORWARD

YEAR 1941		AIRCRAFT		PILOT, OR 1ST PILOT	2ND PILOT, PUPIL OR PASSENGER	DUTY (INCLUDING RESULTS AND REMARKS)
MONTH	DATE	Type	No.			
—	—	—	—	—		— TOTALS BROUGHT FORWARD
Nov	7	BLENHEIM	7307	SELF	Sgt EYRES Sgt KENNEDY	NIGHT FLYING TEST
	7	BLENHEIM	7307	SELF	Sgt EYRES Sgt KENNEY	3 NIGHT LANDINGS
	7	BLENHEIM	7307	SELF	Sgt WHITTLE Sgt KENNEDY	1. NIGHT LANDING
	15	BLENHEIM	7307	SELF	Sgt EYRES Sgt KENNEDY	NIGHT CROSS-COUNTRY BASE - BICESTER - BASE
	15	BLENHEIM	7307	SELF	Sgt EYRES Sgt KENNEDY	NIGHT FLYING TEST
	30	BLENHEIM	7307	SELF	Sgt EYRES Sgt KENNEDY	AIR TEST
		G.H.Jenkins S/LDR O.C. "A" FLIGHT			*J.A.G. Jenkins* W/C O.C. 114 SQUADRON	

GRAND TOTAL [Cols. (1) to (10)]
246 Hrs. 3.0 Mins.

TOTALS CARRIED FORWARD

~ 206 ~

YEAR 1941		AIRCRAFT		PILOT, OR 1ST PILOT	2ND PILOT, PUPIL OR PASSENGER	DUTY (INCLUDING RESULTS AND REMARKS)
MONTH	DATE	Type	No.			
DEC	5	BLENHEIM	7307	SELF	Sgt EYRES Sgt KENNEDY	— TOTALS BROUGHT FORWARD Z.Z LANDING
	7	BLENHEIM	7307	SELF	Sgt EYRES Sgt KENNEDY	FORMATION AND N.F. TEST
	7	BLENHEIM	7307	SELF	Sgt EYRES Sgt KENNEDY	OPERATION ON DOCKS AT OSTEND 9000 FT
	9	BLENHEIM	6264	SELF	Sgt EYRES Sgt KENNEDY	BOMBING TEST
	9	BLENHEIM	6264	SELF	Sgt EYRES Sgt KENNEDY	BOMBING TEST
	11	BLENHEIM	6262	S/L POLLARD	Sgt LYON SELF	BASE – PREDANNACK
	15	BLENHEIM	7307	SELF	Sgt EYRES Sgt KENNEDY	LOW LEVEL FORMATION
	15	BLENHEIM	7307	SELF	Sgt EYRES Sgt KENNEDY	LOCAL FORMATION
	16	BLENHEIM	7307	SELF	Sgt EYRES Sgt KENNEDY	LOW FORMATION
	16	BLENHEIM	7307	SELF	Sgt EYRES Sgt KENNEDY	LOCAL FORMATION
	17	BLENHEIM	7307	SELF	Sgt EYRES Sgt KENNEDY	LOW FORMATION
	22	BLENHEIM	7307	SELF	Sgt EYRES Sgt KENNEDY	FORMATION TO DRIFFIELD

GRAND TOTAL [Cols. (1) to (10)]

258 Hrs. 40 Mins.

TOTALS CARRIED FORWARD

Year 1941		Aircraft		Pilot, or 1st Pilot	2nd Pilot, Pupil or Passenger	Duty (Including Results and Remarks)
MONTH	DATE	Type	No.			
—	—	—	—	—		—— Totals Brought Forward
DEC	23	BLENHEIM	7307	SELF	Sgt EYRES Sgt KENNEDY	FORMATION DRIFFIELD - LOSSIEMOUTH
	27	BLENHEIM	7307	SELF	Sgt EYRES Sgt KENNEDY	OPERATION TO HERDLA 250 RUNWAYS HIT. ME 109s DESTROYED Co-OPERATION WITH COMMANDOS
	28	BLENHEIM	7307	SELF	Sgt EYRES Sgt KENNEDY	LOSSIEMOUTH - BASE

J.H. Hewkins S/LR
OC. "A" FLIGHT

J.H. Jenkins W/C
OC 114 SQUADRON

GRAND TOTAL [Cols. (1) to (10)]
...2.6.8....Hrs. 45...Mins.

Totals Carried Forward

YEAR 1942		AIRCRAFT		PILOT, OR 1ST PILOT	2ND PILOT, PUPIL OR PASSENGER	DUTY (INCLUDING RESULTS AND REMARKS)
MONTH	DATE	Type	No.			
—	—	—	—	—		TOTALS BROUGHT FORWARD
JAN	24	BLENHEIM	7307	SELF	Sgt EYRES Sgt KENNEDY	NIGHT FLYING TEST
	27	BLENHEIM	7307	SELF	Sgt EYRES Sgt KENNEDY	N.F. TEST
	28	BLENHEIM	7307	SELF	Sgt EYRES Sgt KENNEDY	NIGHT OPERATIONS TO SCHIPOL AERODROME ABANDONED DUE TO PORT ENGINE TROUBLE
	30	BLENHEIM	7307	SELF	Sgt EYRES Sgt KENNEDY	AIR TEST

J?H?skelly S/LDR
O.C. "A" FLIGHT

J?H? Jenkins W/C
O.C. 114TH SQUADRON

| | GRAND TOTAL [Cols. (1) to (10)] 271 Hrs. 45 Mins. | | | | | TOTALS CARRIED FORWARD |

Abortive trip to Schipol on 28th January (see page 41)

YEAR 1942		AIRCRAFT		PILOT, OR 1ST PILOT	2ND PILOT, PUPIL OR PASSENGER	DUTY (INCLUDING RESULTS AND REMARKS)
MONTH	DATE	Type	No.			
—	—	—	—	—		TOTALS BROUGHT FORW...
FEB	7	BLENHEIM	7307	SELF	Sgr EYRES Sgr KENNEDY	LOCAL FORMATION. No...
	8	BLENHEIM	7307	SELF	Sgr EYRES Sgr KENNEDY	LOCAL FORMATION N....
	10	BLENHEIM	7307	SELF	Sgr EYRES Sgr KENNEDY	BASE — WATTISHAM
	10	BLENHEIM	7307	SELF	Sgr EYRES Sgr KENNEDY	WATTISHAM — BASE
	12	BLENHEIM	7307	SELF	Sgr EYRES Sgr KENNEDY	SEARCH FOR GNEISENAU AND SCHARNHORST SIGHTED AT DR. $51°50'N$ $03°40'E$ AT 400'. NO ATTACK MADE DUE TO PORT ENGINE KU... U/S INTENSE LIGHT AND HEAVY FLAK
	13	BLENHEIM	N3613	SELF	Sgr EYRES Sgr KENNEDY	AIR TEST
	14	BLENHEIM		SELF	Sgr EYRES Sgr KENNEDY	LOCAL FORMATION. N.L.
	15	BLENHEIM	7307	SELF	Sgr EYRES Sgr KENNEDY	LOCAL FORMATION. No...
	16	BLENHEIM	7307	SELF	Sgr EYRES Sgr KENNEDY	NIGHT TEST

GRAND TOTAL [Cols. (1) to (10)]
280 Hrs. 40 Mins.   · TOTALS CARRIED FORW...

Search for the Scharnhorst and Gneisenau (see page 42)

YEAR 1942		AIRCRAFT		PILOT, OR 1ST PILOT	2ND PILOT, PUPIL OR PASSENGER	DUTY (INCLUDING RESULTS AND REMARKS)
MONTH	DATE	Type	No.			
—	—	—	—	—	—	— Totals Brought Forward
FEB	16	BLENHEIM	7307	SELF	Sgt EYRES Sgt KENNEDY	NIGHT OPERATIONS SOESTERBURG AERODROME. FLARE PATH BOMBED FROM 700'. NO FLAK. PORT ENGINE CUT OVER TARGET
	23	BLENHEIM	7307	SELF	Sgt EYRES Sgt KENNEDY CPL WOOD	AIR TEST
	24	BLENHEIM	7307	SELF	Sgt EYRES Sgt KENNEDY	LOCAL FORMATION No I.
	27	BLENHEIM	7307	SELF	Sgt EYRES Sgt KENNEDY	AIR TEST
	28	BLENHEIM	7307	SELF	Sgt EYRES Sgt KENNEDY	LOW LEVEL FORMATION I.
	28	BLENHEIM	6510	SELF	Sgt EYRES Sgt KENNEDY	CIRCUS TO OSTEND AT 10000 DOCKS HIT INTENSE FLAK. VERY ACCURATE
	28	BLENHEIM	5759	SELF	Sgt EYRES Sgt KENNEDY	AIR TEST

J.A. Hewson S/LDR
O.C. "A" FLIGHT

J.A. Hewson W/C
O.C. 114 SQDN

GRAND TOTAL [Cols. (1) to (10)]
291 Hrs. 10 Mins.

TOTALS CARRIED FORWARD

Year 1942		Aircraft		Pilot, or 1st Pilot	2nd Pilot, Pupil or Passenger	Duty (Including Results and Remarks)
Month	Date	Type	No.			
—	—	—	—	—		— Totals Brought Forward
Mar	3	Blenheim	7307	SELF	Sgt Eyres Sgt Kennedy	Night Test.
	3	"	6264	SELF	Sgt Eyres Sgt Kennedy	Night Test
	3	"	6264	SELF	Sgt Eyres Sgt Kennedy	Night Ops Recalled
	8	"	6032	SELF	Sgt Eyres Sgt Kennedy	High Level Bombing
	8	"	7307	SELF	Sgt Eyres Sgt Kennedy	Night Test
	10	"	3613	SELF	Sgt Eyres Sgt Kennedy	Night Test
	10	"	3613	SELF	Sgt Eyres Sgt Kennedy	2 Night Landings
	13	"	7319	SELF	Sgt Eyres Sgt Kennedy	Night Test
	16	"	7307	SELF	Sgt Eyres Sgt Kennedy	Air Test
	17		2224	SELF	Sgt Eyres Sgt Kennedy	Night Test
	18		7307	SELF	Sgt Eyres Sgt Kennedy	Air Test
	23	"	7307	SELF	Sgt Eyres Sgt Kennedy	Night Test
	24	"	7319	SELF	Sgt Eyres Sgt Kennedy	Base - Lossiemouth

GRAND TOTAL [Cols. (1) to (10)]

" .....301.....Hrs. .....40.....Mins.

Totals Carried Forward

YEAR 1942		AIRCRAFT		PILOT, OR 1ST PILOT	2ND PILOT, PUPIL OR PASSENGER	DUTY (INCLUDING RESULTS AND REMARKS)
MONTH	DATE	Type	No.			
—	—	—	—	—	Sgt EYRES Sgt KENNEDY	TOTALS BROUGHT FORWARD AIR TEST
MAR	27	BLENHEIM	7319	SELF		
	29	"	7319	SELF	Sgt EYRES Sgt KENNEDY	OPERATIONAL WEATHER RECC NORTH OF SHETLANDS
	30	"	7319	SELF	Sgt EYRES Sgt KENNEDY	OPERATIONAL WEATHER RECC OFF NORWEGIAN COAST

[signature] S/LDR
O.C "A" FLIGHT.

[signature] S/LD
"OC" 114 SQDN

MAR 28 Z7307, my faithful "L" did not return from night operations on Schipol — F/Sgt Popplestone was flying her.

APRIL	1	BLENHEIM	7319	SELF	Sgt EYRES Sgt KENNEDY	AIR-SEA RESCUE OFF SHETLANDS
"	1	BLENHEIM	7319	SELF	Sgt EYRES Sgt KENNEDY	A.S.R CLOSE IN SHETLANDS
	3	BLENHEIM	7319	SELF	Sgt EYRES Sgt KENNEDY	LOSSIEMOUTH – BASE
	14	BLENHEIM	7319	SELF	Sgt EYRES Sgt KENNEDY	PRACTISE BEAM APPROACH

GRAND TOTAL [Cols. (1) to (10)]
...3.2.3...Hrs...5.0...Mins.

TOTALS CARRIED FORWARD

Gordon records the loss of his faithful Blenheim 'L' for London.

YEAR 1942		AIRCRAFT		PILOT, OR 1ST PILOT	2ND PILOT, PUPIL OR PASSENGER	DUTY (INCLUDING RESULTS AND REMARKS)
MONTH	DATE	Type	No.			
—	—	—	—	—	Sgt EYRES Sgt KENNEDY	TOTALS BROUGHT FORWARD
APRIL	15	BLENHEIM	7319	SELF		NIGHT OPS SOESTERBURG
						INACTIVE. BOMBED A/D
						No FLAK. SOME S/Ls.
	16	BLENHEIM	8800	SELF	Sgt EYRES	HIGH LEVEL BOMBING
	18	BLENHEIM	7319	SELF	Sgt EYRES Sgt KENNEDY	NIGHT Q TEST
	19	BLENHEIM	7319	SELF	Sgt EYRES Sgt KENNEDY	AIR TEST
	21	BLENHEIM	7319	SELF	Sgt EYRES Sgt KENNEDY	FORMATION. No I.
	23	BLENHEIM	7319	SELF	Sgt EYRES Sgt KENNEDY	FORMATION No I.
	27	BLENHEIM	7319	SELF	Sgt EYRES Sgt KENNEDY	BASE - TANGMERE
	28	BLENHEIM	7319	SELF	Sgt EYRES Sgt KENNEDY	TANGMERE - BASE
	29	BLENHEIM	7319	SELF	Sgt EYRES Sgt KENNEDY	FORMATION No I.
	29	BLENHEIM	7319	SELF	Sgt EYRES Sgt KENNEDY	BOMBED Runways SCHIPOL A/D 20 S/Ls. SLIGHT FLAK
	30	BLENHEIM	7319	SELF	Sgt EYRES Sgt KENNEDY	PRACTISE CIRCUS FORMATION LED No 2. V.c.

GRAND TOTAL [Cols. (1) to (10)]

338 Hrs. 45 Mins.

TOTALS CARRIED FORWARD

Night op to Soesterburg on April 15th (see page 45)

~ 214 ~

YEAR 1942		AIRCRAFT		PILOT, OR 1ST PILOT	2ND PILOT, PUPIL OR PASSENGER	DUTY (INCLUDING RESULTS AND REMARKS)
MONTH	DATE	Type	No.			
—	—	—	—	—	—	TOTALS BROUGHT FORWARD

[signature] S/LDR
O.C. "A" FLIGHT

[signature] W/CDR
O.C. "114" SQDN.

YEAR 1942		AIRCRAFT		PILOT, OR 1ST PILOT	2ND PILOT, PUPIL OR PASSENGER	DUTY (INCLUDING RESULTS AND REMARKS)
MAY	6	BLENHEIM	6446	SELF	F/SGT EYRES SGT KENNEDY	A & E TEST
"	6	— " —	6811	SELF	F/SGT EYRES SGT KENNEDY	BASE - HALTON - BASE
"	8	— " —	6811	SELF	F/SGT EYRES	AIR TEST LOOPED THE LOOP.
"	16	— " —	5635	SELF	F/SGT EYRES SGT KENNEDY	NORTHOLT - BASE
"	10	— " —	5635	SELF	F/SGT EYRES SGT KENNEDY	A & E TEST
"	17	— " —	6337	SELF	F/SGT EYRES SGT KENNEDY	PRACTISE BOMBING
"	17	— " —	7319	SELF		AIR TEST
"	18	— " —	7319	SELF		N.F.T.
	19	— " —	7319			N.F.T.

GRAND TOTAL [Cols. (1) to (10)]
...345... Hrs. ...30... Mins.

TOTALS CARRIED FORWARD

| YEAR 1942 | | AIRCRAFT | | PILOT, OR | 2ND PILOT, PUPIL | DUTY |
MONTH	DATE	Type	No.	1ST PILOT	OR PASSENGER	(INCLUDING RESULTS AND REMARKS)
—	—	—	—	—	F/SGT EYRES Sgt KENNEDY	— TOTALS BROUGHT FORWARD
	20	BLENHEIM	7319	SELF	F/SGT EYRES Sgt KENNEDY	N.F.T. ARMY Co-op
	21	— ·· —	7319	SELF	F/SGT EYRES Sgt KENNEDY	ARMY Co-op
	24	— ·· —	7319	SELF	F/SGT EYRES Sgt KENNEDY	BASE — ODIHAM
	25	— ·· —	7319	SELF	F/SGT EYRES Sgt KENNEDY	ARMY Co-op
	25	— ·· —	7319	SELF	F/SGT EYRES Sgt KENNEDY	ARMY Co-op
	26	— ·· —	7317	SELF	F/SGT EYRES Sgt KENNEDY	ARMY Co-op
	27	— ·· —	7319	SELF	F/SGT EYRES Sgt KENNEDY	ODIHAM — BASE
	29	— ·· —	7319	SELF	F/SGT EYRES Sgt KENNEDY	N.F.T.
	30	— · —	7319	SELF	F/SGT EYRES Sgt KENNEDY	Ops. BONN. A.D. 3000'. 1000 Ac. BOMBED COLOGNE.

(signature) S/LDR "OC" "A" FLIGHT

(signature) W/COR "OC" 114 SQDN.

GRAND TOTAL [Cols. (1) to (10)]
353 Hrs. 05 Mins.

TOTALS CARRIED FORWARD

The first of the 'Thousand Bomber Raids' – target Cologne – on May 30th (see page 55)

| YEAR 1942 | | AIRCRAFT | | PILOT, OR | 2ND PILOT, PUPIL | DUTY |
MONTH	DATE	Type	No.	1ST PILOT	OR PASSENGER	(INCLUDING RESULTS AND REMARKS)
		—	—	—		TOTALS BROUGHT FORWARD
JUNE	1	BLENHEIM	7319	SELF	F/SGT EYRES SGT KENNEDY	N. F. TEST
	1	BLENHEIM	7319	SELF	F/SGT EYRES SGT KENNEDY	1000 AC. ON ESSEN. BOMBED ARDORF A/D 3000' PORT ENGINE CUTTING FOR LAST 250 MLS.
	11	BLENHEIM	7319	SELF	F/SGT EYRES SGT KENNEDY	ENG. TEST. PORT CUT
	16	..	7319	SELF	F/SGT EYRES SGT KENNEDY	ENG TEST PORT CUT
	17	..	7319	SELF	F/SGT EYRES SGT KENNEDY	ENG TEST STARB CUT
	17	..	6510	SELF	F/SGT EYRES SGT KENNEDY	FORMATION L.L.
	21	..	7319	SELF	P/O VALLÉ JONES SGT KENNEDY	ENG TEST STARB CUT
	24	..	7319	SELF	F/SGT EYRES SGT KENNEDY	ENG TEST STARB GUI.
		Robert Heakworth F/L /a S/L				O.C. 'A' FLIGHT
		Holland				W/C C.O. 114 Squadron.
		GRAND TOTAL [Cols. (1) to (10)] 363 Hrs. 40 Mins.				TOTALS CARRIED FORWARD

The second of the Thousand Bomber Raids – target Essen – June 1st.

YEAR		AIRCRAFT		PILOT, OR	2ND PILOT, PUPIL	DUTY
MONTH	DATE	Type	No.	1ST PILOT	OR PASSENGER	(INCLUDING RESULTS AND REMARKS)
—	—	—	—	—	—	TOTALS BROUGHT FORWARD
				SUMMARY FOR AUGUST		ANSON
				UNIT.	13. OTU.	
				DATE.	22·9·42	
				SIGNATURE.	F. Shrimpton.	"OC" D FLIGHT
					N/C	
				"C.I" 13. OTU.		
SEP	4	BLENHEIM	3874	SELF	—	FORMATION. No.1
	5	"	3891	"	—	FORMATION. No.1
	5	"	3871	"	P/O DEEKS	FORMATION No.1
	6	"	6100	"	P/O HART	ARMY Co-op
	6	"	6100	"	P/O HART	ARMY Co-op
	8	"	8869	"	—	A & E TEST
	11	"	1798	"	P/O ROBSON F/SGT MOORE	A.S.R. OFF FRENCH COAST
	22	"	1798	"	—	FINMERE & RETURN

GRAND TOTAL [Cols. (1) to (10)]
452 Hrs. 35 Mins.   TOTALS CARRIED FORWARD

SINGLE-ENGINE AIRCRAFT				MULTI-ENGINE AIRCRAFT						PASS-ENGER	INSTR./CLOUD FLYING [Incl. in cols. (1) to (10)]	
DAY		NIGHT		DAY			NIGHT					
DUAL	PILOT	DUAL	PILOT	DUAL	1ST PILOT	2ND PILOT	DUAL	1ST PILOT	2ND PILOT		DUAL	PILOT
(1)	(2)	(3)	(4)	(5)	(6)	(7)	(8)	(9)	(10)	(11)	(12)	(13)
24.50	25.45			3520.	246.45		4.30	27.00		25.45	13.40	28.50.
					1.10							

(*4690—117) Wt. 51983—5030 48,500 4/40 T.S. 700   FORM 414 (A)

On Posting

SUMMARY of FLYING and ASSESSMENTS FOR YEAR COMMENCING 1st. 9 · 7 · *1942

[*For Officer, insert "JUNE" ; For Airman Pilot, insert "AUGUST."]

	S.E. AIRCRAFT		M.E. AIRCRAFT		TOTAL for year	GRAND TOTAL All Service Flying
	Day	Night	Day	Night		
DUAL						64.40
PILOT			165.05	24.30	189.35	300.10
PASSENGER	—	—	—	—		

ASSESSMENT of ABILITY

(To be assessed as :—Exceptional, Above the Average, Average, or Below the Average)

(I) AS A L.B. †PILOT _____ ABOVE THE AVERAGE

(II) AS PILOT–NAVIGATOR/~~NAVIGATOR~~ _____ ABOVE THE AVERAGE

(III) IN BOMBING _____ N/A

(IV) IN AIR GUNNERY _____ N/A

†Insert :—"F.", "L.B.", "G.R.", "F.B.", etc.

ANY POINTS IN FLYING OR AIRMANSHIP WHICH SHOULD BE WATCHED.

Date July 11/42.   Signature _____ Holland _____ W/Cdr.

Officer Commanding 114 Squadron, RAF.

24.50	25.45			3520	24.55		4.30	27.00		25.45	13.40	28.50
(1)	(2)	(3)	(4)	(5)	(6)	(7)	(8)	(9)	(10)	(11)	(12)	(13)

SUMMARY OF FLYING & ASSESSMENT FOR PERIOD FROM 8/1.43 **TO** 24.7.

	S.E. AIRCRAFT		M.E AIRCRAFT		TOTAL FOR PERIOD	GRAND TOTAL ALL FLYING
	DAY	N'GHT	DAY	NIGHT		
DUAL	—	—	16·10	1·30	17·40	
PILOT	—	—	32·15	1·15	33·30	543·05
PASSENGER						

TOTAL HOURS AS FLYING INSTRUCTOR ....

ASSESSMENT OF ABILITY.

EXCEPTIONAL
ABOVE AVERAGE
AVERAGE
or
BELOW THE
AVERAGE

(i) As Pilot *Above Average*

(ii) As Flying Instructor *Average Cat:*

(iii) B.A. Instructor *Average Ability*

ANY SPECIAL REMARKS. *Night Flying - Average*

Signature *C.W.S.Thomas* S/L

Date 19 FEB 1943 **For Officer Comdg No 3 Flying Instructors' School**

One of the author's assessments as an instructor.

Gordon exploring Southern India with his wife Wendy – over 50 years after the war.

Gordon in later years, touring Egypt.